Rosa Parks
Young Rebel

by Kathleen Kudlinski

ALADDIN PAPERBACKS

New York London Toronto Sydney Singapore

First Aladdin Paperbacks edition January 2001

Text copyright © 2001 by Kathleen Kudlinski
Illustrations copyright © 2001 by Meryl Henderson

Aladdin Paperbacks
An imprint of Simon & Schuster
Children's Publishing Division
1230 Avenue of the Americas
New York, NY 10020

The text for this book was set in Adobe Garamond.

Printed and bound in the United States of America

6 8 10 9 7 5

Library of Congress Catalog Card Number: 00-111092

ISBN: 0-689-83925-1

Illustrations

Contents

Rosa Parks

Young Rebel

Uppity Girl

"Hey, you!"

Rosa McCauley hurried her little brother along. She did not turn around. Rosa knew this white boy's voice. Franklin often picked on them as they walked home from school. "Don't stop," she urged Sylvester.

"What's the matter? You coloreds can't hear?" Rosa heard the boy's footsteps on the dirt road behind her. "Or are y'all just stupid?"

There were no houses on this stretch of road; just scrubby pine woods and cotton fields, red clover and poison ivy. Everything they passed was dusty and wilting in the autumn heat.

Rosa could hear Franklin breathing close now. *Go away,* she wished. *Just go.* There wasn't anybody meaner in the whole town of Pine Level, she thought. Maybe in all of Alabama. Why was he always picking on her? She walked on, faster now, holding herself tall. Inside her head, she said Bible verses for strength.

"Uppity, ain't ya?"

Rosa kept her eyes ahead. Sylvester was crowding near to her, his arm brushing the skirt of her dress. He stumbled as he tried to make his short legs keep up with hers.

"Slow down some," he whimpered.

"Run, little nigger!" Franklin shouted. He didn't have to yell it. The hate word slammed into Rosa's mind and burned in her gut.

Beside Rosa, Sylvester tripped. His knee hit an old brick on the road.

"Ouch!" he yelped.

"Oh, baby fall down." Franklin laughed cruelly. "Do he want another boo-boo?"

Rosa whipped around, her dark eyes flashing.

"Don't you dare touch my brother!"

"Oh, ho. Now who's talking proud! I just want to help." But the look on Franklin's face meant more trouble. He made a fist and took a step toward them. Before she could think, Rosa picked up the brick that had tripped her brother.

"Leave us be!" she yelled, and brought the brick up by her head, ready to throw. Rosa was trembling all through with anger. Franklin wasn't going to get away with it—not today. "Go home!" She snarled.

"You couldn't hurt me with that ol' brick," Franklin said. His words were brave, but his pale eyes were wide with surprise. "You're just a girl." He was stalling, Rosa could tell. "And," he said, his voice getting louder, "a scrawny nigger girl at that."

The word dug into her.

"I been pickin' cotton all fall," Rosa said, "I may be little, but my arm's as strong as your's has ever been!" She pulled the brick back as if to throw it into his face.

She watched Franklin's eyes narrow as he looked at her arm. Rosa held her breath. "I ain't going to get into it with no ten year old," Franklin told her. He took a step back and looked quickly around him.

He's looking for help, Rosa thought. She forced herself not to smile. She knew she was small for her age. And she was black, too. But she had threatened Franklin. And he was backing off! Rosa stood as tall as she ever had in her life. She felt Sylvester's hand grab hers.

"Wouldn't be fair to fight a girl, nohow," Franklin said. Rosa knew he was just saying it to make himself feel better. He backed down the road, his eyes never leaving the brick in her hand. "You just watch yourself," he threatened. Finally, he turned and stalked away.

A mockingbird sang in the silence. Rosa let herself grin. She reached down and hugged Sylvester tight. "Time we be going home," she told him, brushing off his dusty coveralls. "I can't wait till Mama hears what I did to Big Bad Franklin."

"You mean to tell me that you stood right up to that white boy?" Mrs. McCauley's hands were

on her hips, her face set and hard. The cackling of chickens floated through the open door of their little farmhouse.

"Yes, ma'am, I did." Rosa grinned at her mother. She set her school papers on the table and went on. "He made a fist like he would hit me, so I picked up a brick. I even made like I might hit him." The look on her mother's face stopped her. Rosa bit her lip.

"Sylvester," Mama said, her voice low, "go get some wood for the stove. Mind you don't fetch yourself a snake instead."

Sylvester looked at Rosa, then slunk out the door like a dog that had been kicked.

When he was gone, Mrs. McCauley's quiet anger filled the little wooden house.

"I didn't throw it at him, Mama, honest I didn't."

Mrs. McCauley was still silent. "Mama," Rosa said, "that boy stopped bothering me right there and then." It had felt so good to watch Franklin back down. She stood straighter, just thinking about it.

"Rosa Louise McCauley," Mama's voice filled

the living room. "Are you crazy? You must never, never do that again."

Rosa looked at her mother's face and felt all of her pride draining away into the dirt floor beneath her feet. Tears filled her eyes. She started to explain. "But, Mama . . ." Rosa knew not to bother finishing her sentence. Mrs. McCauley was not in a listening mood.

"If any white—boy or girl, man or woman—gives you trouble, Rosa, you make your eyes look down. You be polite. You don't even think to hit back. And you never answer back."

Every word hit Rosa's gut like a fist. "That's not fair, Mama!" she said.

"No, it's not. But that's how we have to live." Mrs. McCauley sat down like she was suddenly all worn out. "That's how it's been since February 4, 1913, the very day you were born in Tuskeegee. It's that way all over Alabama. Far as I know, that's how it is everywhere this side of heaven."

"It's not right!"

"Franklin can hurt you, Rosa. Or, next time,

maybe his white friends or his papa comes. They can hit you. Or they can do worse, much, much worse." Mama shook her head. "Remember the men who were hung back last year? White people did those lynchings."

Mama sighed. "The police did nothin', Rosa. They never do—not for us coloreds. White murderers will never see justice until Judgment Day."

Rosa pictured a man from their church. They had found him one morning, hanging from a tree, dead. Whites had done it. "Don't tell me anymore, Mama!"

"Rosa, is that you, sassing your mama?" Grandma Rose stormed in from the kitchen. Her back was stiff, her voice tight, her eyes full of fire, and she had the switch in her hand.

"No, ma'am," Rosa said quickly.

"Rosa, here, does not like the idea of turning the other cheek to whites," Mama said.

"She doesn't, does she?" The old lady turned to Rosa. "You thank the Lord, girl, that you are living in 1921. It wasn't that easy for me."

Rosa's shoulders fell. Her grandmother had

been born a slave. Why hadn't she held her tongue?

"I'm sorry, Grandma Rose," she said. "I forgot."

"You just sit yourself down, girl. We are going to have us a little talk while your mama finishes dinner." Rosa's grandmother stared at Mrs. McCauley. "The beans need stirring, Leona, and you need to pack." Rosa sniffed the air. The scent of sweet potato pie was beginning to float from the kitchen. Her stomach growled.

"Is it time for Mama to leave again?" she sighed. It was good that her mother had a teaching job in a nearby town, but she why did she have to live there, too?

"Think, Rosa," Grandma Rose eased her tired bones into a chair. She set the switch on the table and leaned across to bring her face close to Rosa's. "Your great-grandmother was whipped whenever her owner felt like it," she said. "She was fed when her owner decided to spare her the food." The old woman's voice was rising. "My mama was never given shoes, so she lived her whole life barefoot."

Rosa sat quietly, her eyes down, listening. How could she have felt bad about a little problem like Franklin's smart mouth? "Your great-grandmother," the old woman went on, "was a slave. No education. She had no choices at all. Now, here you are, with plenty to eat, school every day, and living on land we own." She glared at Rosa. "How dare you say, 'It's not fair?'"

Rosa felt like crying. It would have hurt less if Grandmother had just used the switch on her.

"My mama was a slave," Grandmother went on, "and she was a good woman, strong and proud and full of faith." Rosa waited quietly while Grandmother told the old story, then leaned forward and spread her hands on the wooden table. The good part was coming. "Then President Lincoln set us free," Grandmother said. "I was four. Mama and Daddy were free, and so was I. No more whippings, praise the Lord."

"That's when your Daddy made this table, right?" Rosa prompted.

"With his own hands." Grandmother said. "He carved the pegs to hold it together and fitted them in, tight as nails, so we'd have a proper table to eat on. I can still remember his voice saying grace every meal. . . ." Grandmother's words trailed off. Rosa tried to imagine how many blessings had been said over the table. All of her life, Grandma Rose had read the Bible to them at the table before meals; then Grandfather had prayed. Rosa could almost feel the Holy Spirit alive in the warm, brown wood.

"Time to clean up for dinner, Rosa. Your granddaddy will be home soon." Grandma Rose pushed herself to her feet. "You best not be telling him about that Franklin boy. You don't want to get him riled up."

Rosa swallowed. Grandmother was right. Grandfather hated whites more than anybody she knew. But it made sense. She walked out into the yard, trying not to think about the stories he'd told of being a slave boy. The beatings. The table scraps he'd gotten to eat—when he was lucky.

"Sylvester!" she called to her brother. That was Grandfather's name, too, Rosa thought with a start. She hoped her brother wouldn't get the fiery temper as well. Maybe he wouldn't if she could keep boys like Franklin from bothering him.

Franklin. The name made her burn inside again. He had no right to pick on them like that. But maybe Mama and Grandma Rose were right. Perhaps there wasn't anything she could do about it. "Sylvester!" she called again. Her brother hurried from the field, scattering chickens as he ran.

All she could do, Rosa decided, was be good and strong and proud, like Grandma Rose had said, and she would be full of faith, too.

Rosa sat another moment at the table, picturing Franklin walking down the road away from her. She straightened in the chair. For just a few minutes there on that road, she had felt so good. Even if Grandma Rose and Mama were right, there had to be a way to change things. *Someday,* she promised herself, *things will be better.*

Two Schools

"Please, Mama," Rosa whispered. It hurt to talk aloud. "I really want to go."

"You look right poorly, Rosa." Mama held her hand on Rosa's forehead. "I don't want you to get run down again."

Rosa tried to swallow, but it hurt too much. "I don't feel any worse than usual," she said. It was true. Rosa's tonsils were often infected. "And it's nice out." She pointed through the window. Sunshine made the leaves glow on the pecan tree. Rosa sighed. "Mama, I don't want to repeat another year of school." It was bad enough to be in fifth grade again. If she had to stay home every time she felt sick, she'd never make it to sixth grade! And it was all because of her tonsils. She squeezed her eyes shut and forced herself to swallow.

"Take another biscuit with you then to eat on the way." Mama said. "You need to keep up your strength."

Rosa and Sylvester headed toward school, walking on the side of the road. When cars whipped past, Rosa held her loose cotton dress down so the dusty wind couldn't blow its skirt up. Sylvester threw a stone at a bluejay that was scolding from a fence post. "Sylvester," Rosa whispered warningly. Her brother grinned and skipped ahead. Rosa tried to keep up, but ran out of breath. The morning was still cool, but the walk felt long today.

"Sylvester," she croaked. Her brother waited for her to catch up. She offered him the biscuit.

He stared at it for a long moment. "Don't you want it?"

Rosa pointed at her throat and shook her head.

Sylvester bit into Rosa's snack as the big yellow school bus drove past in a swirl of dust. Half a dozen white children leaned out of the windows. "Get off our road, pickaninnies!" a boy's voice threatened from the bus. "Ain't they cute?" a girl's shrill voice teased. "Uppity coloreds!" someone else yelled. An apple core landed at Rosa's feet. "Who's the Chinese?" another boy shouted. Rude laughter floated from the bus. At last it was gone. The grit settled in new patterns in the road.

Rosa looked at Sylvester. His face was even paler than usual as he stared at the dust-covered biscuit. "Who they calling Chinese?" he asked.

Sylvester's eyes were a little slanted, Rosa thought, but it made him look cute. And his skin was paler than anybody else at the black school. That was a fact. But there was no call to tease him about it. *As if the white kids needed a reason to be mean,* Rosa reminded herself. "Pay them no mind," she told her brother.

Sylvester brushed most of the grit off the rest of the biscuit and ate it in one bite. "Why do white children get a bus to ride to school?" he grumbled.

"Don't you talk with your mouth full," Rosa scolded. They walked awhile. Only the sound of a meadowlark singing from the fence by the cotton field broke the silence. Finally Rosa answered, "They need a bus because their school is farther away."

"No, it's not." Sylvester mumbled. "I saw it from Grandfather's wagon. Their school is big and brick and painted all white. The door has a screen, and there's even glass in the windows. There's grass in the yard and flowers and swings hanging from pipes."

Her brother's words made Rosa imagine what it would be like to be allowed to go to Pine Level School. She'd passed it, too, and had stared through the windows. She'd seen the bright maps and colorful charts on the walls, and teachers passing out piles of fresh, clean paper to the students. The white children always seemed to have new books, too. She shook her head to clear out the wicked envy that was growing there. *Thou shalt not covet,* she told herself sternly. It was a blessing that they had a school to go to in Pine Level. Not every town had one for black students.

Sylvester kicked at loose stones as he walked beside her. "Grandfather said he pays the taxes that go to run that white school. He said it's a crime coloreds aren't even allowed inside the school they paid for." Sylvester's little voice sounded like Grandfather's, hard and angry.

Rosa thought quickly. "Yes, it is pretty," she said, "but do you know they have to go to school for nine whole months?" She tried to make it sound miserable. "The whites have to sit indoors and be good and quiet while we are outside, doing what we want."

"You telling me true?" Sylvester's feet plodded down the road in time with hers.

"Yes," Rosa said. She didn't say that their school, the Spring Hill Church School, started late just so the colored children could work in the cotton fields in the fall. She didn't say it let out early so the coloreds could weed the cotton seedlings in the spring either. Instead, she said, "Sylvester, we get to be out, listening to birds and playing and fishing. All those months, white children have to sit still with their legs tucked under those silly little desks."

"Is that why they are so mean to us?" Sylvester asked.

Rosa shrugged. "My throat hurts too much to talk anymore." She tried to imagine how much more she could learn in an extra four months of school a year. It purely wasn't fair.

Miss Beulah was ringing the bell from the sagging schoolhouse steps, so they had to hurry by the Mount Zion Church to get to the school. "Morning, ma'am," Rosa gasped as she rushed past the teacher. Rosa took her place, panting, on the bench between the only other fifth-grade girl and one of the fourth-grade boys. She tucked her lunch pail beneath her feet. Then Rosa smiled a silent hello to the sixth graders sitting on the bench facing her across the room. How she missed studying with those friends! She made herself calm. If she had missed school too often to keep up with them, God must have had a reason for it.

One last boy dashed into the door and hung his hat on the row of pegs on the wall. Before he slid into his place on the bench, he set a shiny apple on the pot-bellied stove. Every day, gifts like this appeared for Miss Beulah. In the winter, of course, the presents sat on her worn old desk, while a wood fire crackled in the stove.

All the students stood as the gray-haired teacher took her place at the front of the room. Rosa tried to make her hands hang as gracefully as her teacher's. She smoothed her hair, licked her lips, and grinned at the sixth graders again. She loved the moment before school started.

"Good morning, children," Miss Beulah said.

"Good morning, Miss Beulah," they all answered together. It was the only time they called her by her formal name. But the opening ceremony was formal. Rosa bowed her head to join in the morning prayer. "Amen!" Sylvester's voice rang out with the others at the end. Rosa had kept her voice soft. She sang quietly through the hymn, too. Even when her throat felt fine, she wouldn't sing out. She loved the words, but wished she had been given a more beautiful voice with which to praise the Lord. *There would have to be another way to serve, she told herself.*

"Y'all may be seated," Miss Beulah said, then called out, "Opening, please."

Rosa watched her brother stand up with the other fourth graders. They cleared their throats and glanced at each other. Floorboards creaked under their feet and Rosa held her breath. Would Sylvester remember all the words? Memorizing was hard for him. All on her own, Rosa had tried to learn as many Bible verses as she could. That way they came easy to her mind whenever she needed them. All that practice made learning to recite easier for her.

"We the people . . . ," Rosa silently mouthed the words as the fourth graders recited the Preamble to the Constitution. She remembered it, of course, from fourth grade. She had practiced it again with Sylvester to help him get ready for today.

As his class recited the words, he looked often at Rosa. He was watching her lips. *You're supposed to know it without my help!* Rosa scolded silently, and stopped moving her lips. Suddenly Sylvester's eyes got wide. He stumbled over the next few words. Rosa began mouthing them again, and Sylvester made it through to the end.

Rosa shook her head at her brother. *We'll go over it tonight until he really knows it,* she promised herself.

When the opening was done, Miss Beulah gave each grade their assignments. While the first graders were still doing their sums on the blackboard, Rosa finished her reading. Mama had taught Rosa to read before she ever got to school so she often finished ahead of her classmates. She took a moment to look around the classroom. *Where did Mama sit when she came to school here?* she wondered. She stared at the teacher's back and tried to imagine what Miss Beulah had looked like back then. Was she skinny? Did she wear her hair down? In bows? She tried to imagine her teacher's face without wrinkles. She couldn't make the picture in her mind.

Just then, Miss Beulah turned and smiled right at her. Rosa quickly ducked her head and began working on her fractions. She balanced the slate board on her lap as she copied the examples from the chalkboard. Time sped in school for her, as it always did. Soon it was lunchtime, then recess.

Sylvester played ball with the other boys. Rosa joined the girls in a ring. They played "Ring Around the Rosie" for the little girls, then "Rise, Sally, Rise," and "Little Sally Walker, Sitting in the Saucer." Rosa's throat hurt, and she felt dizzy, so she stood to the side for one game. While she watched, a first grader tripped and fell, trying to skip along with the older girls.

All the girls gathered around her, brushing off her dress and giving her hugs. The little girl was brave about her skinned knee and stood quietly while someone retied her sash, but she started to sob when she saw the tear in her skirt. "Mama made it new for me!" she cried. "I ruined it!" All

the girls looked at each other. Nobody would rip a dress out of carelessness. They all knew how much time it took to sew one, and how much new fabric cost. They'd all grown up watching their mothers make clothes for their own families.

Rosa glanced around the circle. Most of her classmates were wearing hand-me-downs, passed from sister to sister or cousin to cousin, treasured and well cared for. Their dresses were patched and repatched. The skirts would some-day be used again, sewn onto other dresses. Finally the cloth would be cut into pieces and stitched into quilts. A new-sewn dress should be saved for church.

Rosa hoped her own children would be care-ful with the clothes she made for them. She loved sewing. It would be such fun to make baby clothes and little dresses and church suits for boys! "Ready?" a girl asked gently. She handed the first grader a soft, worn handker-chief. As the little girl wiped her eyes and nose, Rosa tried to guess what that cloth had once been. A nightgown? A man's shirt? Soon the girls began playing again. When the bell rang, they lined up to go back into the school. The girls straightened each other's hair bows and retied sashes while they waited.

Miss Beulah went over the fifth graders' arithmetic lesson after recess. Rosa had gotten all of the problems adding fractions correct. After they erased their slates and tried multiplying fractions, she knew she could handle the next skill, too. She knew the answers to all the reading questions. Next, Miss Beulah worked with them on another of Rosa's favorite subjects, geography. Last came history, then the fifth graders went back to their seats. Now it was the sixth graders' turn to work with the teacher, and soon school was over.

"Good night, ma'am." Rosa smiled at Miss Beulah as they left. "God bless."

Rosa and Sylvester walked home well off the road, listening for the sound of the white children's bus. Rosa wondered what they had learned in their school today, sitting at those pretty little desks. *It doesn't matter where you study,* she told herself. They was only one Constitution to memorize. The white kids had to learn the same geography and the same fractions. They read the same Bible. They couldn't get better grades than she did. *And nobody,* she thought, *could have a better teacher than Miss Beulah.* She walked home with her head held high.

Sister Rosa

"Hold still, Sylvester!" Rosa struggled with her brother's tie. "We have to get this right."

"Y'all ready?" Grandfather called. "Can't keep the preacher waiting now."

"Hurry," Sylvester whispered as Rosa's fingers fumbled with the knot in his necktie.

"Settle down," Rosa scolded—and she wasn't talking to her brother. Inside her an anger had simmered all week. "'Let not your heart be troubled,'" she scolded herself with a Bible verse. She took a deep breath, her fingers steadied, and the knot slid into place. "Wait. Your hat!" Rosa

handed it to Sylvester as he pushed past her and out the front door.

Her mother and grandmother were already sitting in the wagon, huddled in a cold drizzle. It had rained on-and-off all week. "Geet up, there," Grandfather urged the horse as Rosa and Sylvester jumped on. The family sat in silence on the ride to the church. Grandfather's rheumatism had been bad all winter. One day that very week, he'd finally cut the toes off of his shoes to make walking less painful. It didn't seem to be helping his feet or his temper. And now he had more things to be cranky about

"Someday we are going back to Africa." That was what he had always said when he heard about another black hung by a white, burned, beaten, or just pushed around. Grandfather had promised the family Africa more times than Rosa could remember. Right after the Civil War ended, a few white men had started a hate club. Its goal was to scare everybody who was not white, and unlike themselves, out of the country. They called themselves the Ku Klux Klan.

The members tried to terrorize blacks and Jews and Catholics and Mexicans. They used violence and threats to make each other feel powerful, too, but in fact these men were cowards.

They knew what they were doing was against the law, but they were afraid of getting in trouble. They wore pointed white hoods over their faces and white robes to cover their clothes. That way nobody ever saw who, exactly, was breaking the law. Even lawmen sometimes joined this secret club. They all swore never to tell anyone who else was part of their Klan. They hid under cover of darkness, prowling from house to house in black neighborhoods. They may have looked like silly grown-up Halloween trick-or-treaters, but their "tricks" were murder and fire, whips and clubs and acid. There were no "treats." This sick club did nothing of any good at all.

Branches of this terrorist group had sprung up here and there over the country. There was a group of this Ku Klux Klan right in Montgomery. "Klansmen" had ridden into Pine Level. Sometimes they prowled right past Rosa's house. So far, the McCauleys had not been attacked. Others in town had. Every time Grandfather heard about another "KKK" strike, he talked again of going to Africa.

He had a book about how blacks could go back to the homeland of their ancestors, the slaves. Grandfather read parts of it to the family over and over. Rosa loved the part that said Negroes were the greatest and proudest race that ever lived on earth. Just this past week, the man who wrote this wonderful book had come to Montgomery. Grandfather had dressed in his Sunday finest to go and hear the man who had the answer to all their problems.

When Grandfather walked in, he got a nasty surprise. Instead of welcoming him, the people at the meeting said his skin was too light to look like a real African. They said he could never go back to live there. They did not even want him to stay to hear the speech.

Grandfather had limped home, looking like a storm cloud with sparks crackling all over inside. He'd been that way ever since, and Rosa was angry, too. She was angry at the men for telling Grandfather he couldn't go to Africa after all. She was angry with the Ku Klux Klan for the evil things they did. She was even angry with Grandfather for being so angry it made them all nervous. Most of all she was angry with herself. She just couldn't calm down inside.

The Bible told her to "serve the Lord with gladness" and "come before his presence with singing." Rosa could repeat the whole of Psalm 100, but she was having trouble being glad about anything. Mostly, she was just angry. This, she knew, was no way to be walking into a church.

The McCauley's wagon pulled up in front of the school. One of the first grader's fathers was nailing the loose step down. *I bet white daddies don't have to hammer nails at their school,* Rosa thought, her anger building even further. Grandfather limped slowly as he led the way to the church next door. *And it has to be raining, too,* Rosa thought, as water trickled down her neck. Everything seemed to be adding to her stormy temper.

She was even crankier after the McCauleys had followed Grandfather to the Mount Zion AME Church next door to the school. He was walking as fast as the pain in his joints would allow. It wasn't fast enough for Rosa.

A crowd of neighbors was already gathered inside the church, all dressed in their Sunday best. "Good Morning, Sister Rosa," one woman called to her. When Rosa didn't answer, Grandmother glared at her. Rosa swallowed. No matter how cranky she felt inside, if she showed it in church, Grandmother would take a switch to her. She made her face calm and her voice soft as she answered, "Good Morning, Sister Louise."

"We surely did need this rain," someone else said. Rosa forced a smile and answered, "Yes, indeed, Brother Thomas." Rosa's teeth were clenched tight behind the smile as she settled into the pew and looked around the church.

All the women's hats bobbed as they bent to

pray. Beside them, children squirmed. Fathers sat tall, close to their wives. *Why can't my daddy be here?* Rosa wondered. He'd been gone for a couple of years. "He's out looking for work," Mama said, when Rosa asked. There were few letters, and Mama didn't read them to the family. Mr. McCauley was a carpenter. *He could have nailed down those loose steps in our school.* It made Rosa angry just to think about. *And then he could come to church with us. He could be sitting down right beside me now.*

"Amen!" Grandma Rose called out right next to her, and suddenly everyone was standing. Rosa blinked. She'd missed her uncle's call to worship! Her uncle was a good pastor, and Rosa was proud of him. She liked it when it was his turn to come to this church. She scrambled to her feet, shaking her head to clear out the anger. The first hymn had begun.

People sang, "I Am Bound for the Promised Land," loudly, clapping and swaying in time with the powerful words. Rosa joined in softly. Soon she began singing the hymn right out, her voice lost in the sound that seemed ready to burst open the walls of the little church. By the second verse, worshippers raised their arms, just to feel the happiness hanging thick in the room. The wild joy made Rosa feel light and even a little dizzy. Neighbors in her pew called out "Alleluia!" and Rosa almost did, too, but the hymn was coming to a close. "Praise God!" called a man in the back. "Glory be!" cried a woman from the front.

"Amen," Grandfather's deep voice rumbled from the end of the pew. It seemed everyone had felt the Spirit moving through them.

Now the church filled with the sounds of rustling clothes, scuffling feet, polite coughs, and clearing of throats as everyone sat down. A baby cried and gurgled to silence. Rosa felt her heart slow down. She took a deep breath. The church smelled of damp clothing, hair pomade, perfume, and neighbors. Rosa looked around at all the people and grinned. This time her teeth weren't clenched. She settled into the pew, every muscle relaxed. It felt wonderful, for a change.

The pastor read from the Bible. He talked about the slaves in Egypt. Then he talked about God calling old Moses to lead his people out of slavery. Moses didn't think he could do it. *What will I do?* Moses worried. *What will I say?* "'I will be with thy mouth and teach thee what thou shalt say,'" the preacher read God's answer. Moses trusted God and did exactly what God had taught him to do—and the slaves all had listened and believed. They had all escaped to the Promised Land because Moses had listened, listened to the word of God.

"Preach it, Brother!" a man called out from behind Rosa.

As Rosa watched two elders carrying the basket through the church, she thought about other blacks who'd helped slaves escape to freedom. Before the Civil War, Harriet Tubman had snuck slaves out of the South on the Underground Railroad. She had been a member of the African Methodist Episcopal Church, too. *I could call her Sister Harriet,* Rosa realized. Sojourner Truth and Frederick Douglass were AME members, too. Their powerful speeches had helped free all the other slaves. Rosa wondered if their words, like Moses', came straight from God. *Did they hear the same sermon when they were ten years old?* It gave her shivers to think she went to the same church as these strong, brave people had.

The next hymn was "Let My People Go." The church members sang even louder than before. Rosa sang and swayed and clapped. She never wanted that joyful feeling to end. When the song was over, no one else seemed to want it to stop either. They all just started in singing again. Some in the church danced in joy. Others wept with happiness.

Then everybody grew quiet for the prayer. Rosa's mind became as still as a pool in the pine woods. The pastor prayed for old Amos, whose barn had been burned last night. He prayed for them all, that they would be listening when God told them what He wanted them to do.

Finally, Rosa's uncle raised his arms over everyone. The whole church seemed to hold its breath. Rosa closed her eyes, waiting for the familiar words of benediction. "The Lord bless thee and keep thee . . . ," the pastor began. As his voice rang through the church, Rosa felt the lightness again. It was a quiet in her mind, a calm in her muscles, a cool stillness where the anger had been. She loved this special feeling. She had lost it this week. Now she knew where she could find it again. ". . . and give thee peace," the pastor finished. Then he said a last "Amen." The service was over. Rosa opened her eyes.

And blinked. Everyone was just standing and talking. Rosa wanted to turn time back, to be singing and swaying with joy, to be listening in the deep, quiet peace of God. She looked at the people around her. Her family and neighbors were just talking about everyday things—as if nothing special had happened at all. But as Rosa listened, she began to smile. The church spirit was there in the warmth of their voices and the joy in their eyes.

The rain had stopped by the time the family climbed back into the wagon. "We're going to help old Amos," Mama said firmly. "He needs us all."

"How much help could I be?" Grandfather protested, "with the rhumatiz acting up this bad?"

"If the Klan had picked our barn to burn, Amos would come to help us," Mama argued. "You'll think of something to do to help. You'll see."

Rosa grinned. This was just like the Moses story.

"Stop by the house and I'll pick up the bread." Mama took charge. "Rosa and Sylvester, y'all gather eggs to bring along. We'll boil them up for sandwiches come suppertime."

Rosa thought fast. "Mama, can we spare one chicken for him, too?"

"Yes, bless you, girl. But y'all be sure to find every last egg before you go chasing chickens. There's going to be a crowd there to feed. You mark my words."

Mama was right. When their wagon drove up, the Smith farm was as busy as a church social. Some of the men were already at work, pulling down the charred cross that the Klan members had burned on Amos's front yard. Rosa swallowed and looked away. Other men were building a shelter for Amos's cow. Amos sat in a chair on his front porch. He was a grown man and old, but Amos looked ready to cry.

The wagon rocked as Grandfather got out. Rosa watched him limp slowly to the old man's side. He eased himself down into a chair and started to talk. Rosa saw Amos cover his face. Then Grandfather rested a hand on his shoulder.

"They threw cow plops in the well!" a woman shouted as she poured a bucket of foul water onto the ground. "Those pigs!"

"The well will be sweet again by Easter!" Grandmother announced. "Boys, y'all come here." Soon she had relays organized. Sylvester and the others ran back and forth from the neighbor's spring to Amos's water barrel, carrying buckets of fresh water.

The women cooked a dinner to share and cleaned up Amos's house for him. Rosa worked with another girl, mending a curtain that was ripped down. Half of the time, the neighbors sang hymns. The rest of the time they shared stories and caught up on the news. Rosa couldn't help but smile as she looked out the window at the busy scene. Together the neighbors were undoing everything the Klan had done.

By the time they left, sunset was gathering. Amos's farm was tidy again. The cow had salve on her burns and shelter over her head, Moses had enough bread for days, and six new chickens roamed his front yard. The burnt timbers were cleared away, the yard swept, and a water barrel filled. Grandfather had never left Amos's side, and now both old men were full of smiles.

As the McCauley wagon rolled off toward home, Grandfather began singing in his deep voice. "Oh, freedom, oh, freedom." The old spiritual floated in the heavy night air. "And before I'd be a slave, I'd be buried in my grave," Mama and Grandmother joined in on the chorus, singing, "and go home to my Lord and be free." They sang verse after verse as the tired horse plodded along. Sylvester slumped against

Rosa, tired from the long day. For a while Rosa just listened to the joy in her family's fine voices. Before they got home, Rosa was humming along, too, but softly so Sylvester wouldn't wake up.

Chopping Cotton

"Look, Rosa," Sylvester said. Rosa stood and blinked at the pain in her back. "There's the white children's school bus."

Rosa leaned on her hoe and looked across the cotton field at the road. A yellow bus rumbled past, trailing the sounds of children's laughter. "It's April," her brother said. "I cain't believe they're still going to school."

Rosa twisted, stretching from side to side to ease her stiff muscles, then bent to get back to weeding.

"I hate them," Sylvester said.

Rosa stood again and looked at her brother. His face was twisted with anger. "All they did to you was drive by, Sylvester." Rosa said. "You've no call to be like that. 'Look at the day that the Lord has made.'" She took a deep breath. The smell of gardenias wafted over the field. A gull cried overhead, his wings white against the deep blue sky. The red sandy soil was sun warmed beneath their bare feet.

She looked back at the row of cotton plants they'd worked already this morning. "We've done well." she told him. "We can be proud." Their fresh hoe marks ringed the base of each young cotton plant. The joe-pye weed and sour grass, the strangling morning glories and pigweed, all were gone. They lay chopped to bits, wilting in the hot spring sun. Now the light could reach the new cotton leaves. The rain could go to the cotton roots instead of watering the greedy weeds. "The cotton can grow now," she encouraged her brother.

"So the weevils can eat it?"

Rosa stared at Sylvester. The boll weevil bugs

wouldn't be getting into the cotton until the summertime. That didn't matter now. Why was Sylvester so prickly?

"Y'all git to work!" Rosa jumped and nearly dropped her hoe. Mr. Freeman was glaring at them across the field from the back of a horse. The horse took a few nervous steps, and the white man pulled back on the reins to quiet him. "You 'spect me to pay for your playtime?" he yelled at them.

Rosa ducked her head, raised her hoe, and chopped it into the sandy ground. *Thunk!* a tuft of grass fell. Quick as a flash, she chopped again, smashing a dandelion. Its puffy seeds went flying, but Rosa's hoe was already falling toward the next weed. *Don't look over here,* she silently willed the field overseer.

With one word, Mr. Freeman could cut their pay just as easily as her hoe cut weeds. Rosa knew her mama needed every bit of the fifty cents she could earn this day, plus Sylvester's fifty cents, too. *Chop!* went the hoe, *chop-chop,* thudding into the hard soil. Sylvester's hoe was thumping into the ground again, too. The field around them was full of the soft thumps and thuds of chopping hoes. Moses Hudson had sent word that his cotton needed chopping, and everyone who could lift a hoe had come.

Their family was lucky, Rosa thought. Mama had enough education to teach school and get a regular paycheck. Not as much as a teacher at the white school, of course, but it was still good money. And Mama often brought home apples and peaches and other gifts from her students to share with the family. Other mothers worked cleaning white people's homes and made much less. The McCauleys owned their own farm, so they could grow most of the food they needed. Grandfather took extra eggs, chickens, milk, and calves to town in his wagon to sell or trade, too.

But every bit of the money Rosa and Sylvester earned working on the neighbor's farms helped. Rosa had been a field hand since she was six. She was proud of how she could chop "from can to can't"—from sunup, when you can see in the fields, to sundown, when you can't anymore. But she did get tired. And the sun got so hot sometimes. Rosa's back hurt. She slowed the frantic pace she'd set for chopping. *It was a long time to day's end.* She thought about all the money she must have earned over the years to help. It gave her a good feeling.

She spent another hour chopping, saying Bible verses in her head, then practicing multiplication tables to pass the time. For a long while she just let the feeling of hot sun and motion carry her without thought.

"Snake!" A child screamed across the field. "Mama! Snake!"

Suddenly grown-ups were running toward the child. One grabbed him up in his arms and jumped back. "Rattler!" he shouted. "Watch your feet!" The others raised their hoes and chopped the ground over and over where the child had been.

"It's dead!" one of them finally shouted.

"Praise be!" the answer came across the field.

Rosa glanced down at her bare toes. She

looked around her at the weed-choked cotton field. She remembered being little and feeling that the field went on forever. It seemed that the day did, too. Now she knew to just keep moving and, sooner or later, the rows—and the day— would come to an end. She picked up her hoe again.

Mr. Freeman rode by a couple of times after lunch break. Rosa thought about his children. They were friendly, even to her. They'd invited her to play with them, but she never had. "Don't you even think to go near them," Grandfather had scolded when he heard that Rosa had talked to them. "I don't never want you playing with them or any other white children, you hear?"

The mosquitoes were biting before Mr. Freeman called the day off. Rosa and Sylvester lined up with the others to turn in their hoes and collect their pay. They both got the full fifty cents, and Rosa stuffed the money deep into the pocket of her dress for safekeeping. "It's not enough," Sylvester grumbled. Rosa turned quickly to see if Mr. Freeman had heard, or Old Moses Hudson. But neither man looked up.

"I know," Rosa said, thinking fast, "let's go fishing."

Sylvester's eyes sparkled. "I'll cut the canes!"

"Slow down, Sugar!" Rosa said. "I have to give Mama the money, and see if she even wants fish for dinner."

"You know she will," Sylvester said. And he was right.

"Do you think four poles will be enough?" Sylvester stood, breathless beside the river. In his hand were four bamboo canes, each twice as tall as Grandfather and covered with leaves.

"Sure 'nuff," Rosa said. "That's all the hooks we got anyhow." She reached into her pocket. "I'll string them. You dig the worms."

Rosa sat on the riverbank. Before her, muddy-colored water swirled in a lazy way. Over her head, Spanish moss hung limp from the live oaks. Mosquitoes hummed and Rosa swept her hands along her legs to brush off any little chiggers before they could settle in and bite. Then she began stripping all of the leaves and twigs off the longest cane. She set it down and used a knife to cut a string just as long as the pole. Next, she tied one end of the string to the tip of the pole. The other end of the string was tied to a hook she'd brought from home.

A bluejay shrieked a warning when Rosa stood to look around for a small stick to use as a float. Long, fine pine needles lay sifted over the mud from the spring flood. Here and there were broken twigs and branches that had been swept downstream with the high water. Some were stuck at waist level in the trees where they'd gotten tangled before the river flood went down again. Rosa chose one, dried from days of endless, hot sun, and snapped off a piece as long as her hand. A loop in the string a couple of feet above the hook held this float tight, and the first fishing pole was ready for its bait. Rosa laid it aside. She tied another little piece of driftwood to a shorter string to hold their catch and reached for the next cane.

"I got the worms," Sylvester slid down the bank to join Rosa, an old can held tight in his dirty hands.

"Here's the first pole," Rosa handed it to her brother. "Remember how I showed you to bait the hook?"

Sylvester nodded. As he worked, she began stripping the second cane. She didn't look up when she heard the *Plop!* of his baited hook hitting the water, well out into the stream.

"Where'd you learn?" he asked. A sharp *crack* told Rosa he was making a brace for the first pole.

She thought for a moment as she threaded the string through the eye of the second hook. "I guess it was before you'd remember. You were really little." She handed him the pole and began another. "A nice old white lady used to take us fishing, you and me."

"A nice *white* lady?" Sylvester sounded shocked.

"You really don't remember anything?" Rosa asked. "You used to sit on her lap. And she

showed me how to hold the worm so the hook would slip right in—and not come out. And she used to tickle you, and we would laugh at how you wiggled."

"No," Sylvester said, his voice flat.

"No, what?" Rosa asked and handed him the third pole. She glanced out into the water. "You mind that float out there."

"No white lady ever touched me. You, neither."

"I got no call to lie," Rosa said. "Not only that, but a white soldier once patted my head."

"Now I know you are just spinning yarns," Sylvester told her. "'Sides, why would any soldier ever do that to you?"

"I don't know why. He was old, old. He had fought in Mr. Lincoln's war on the North's side." That was all she could remember about him. "But he said something like 'Ain't you just the cutest one?' and patted me right on the head. Mama and Grandma Rose still talk about it sometimes."

Sylvester was shaking his head. "You're making this up."

"You ask Mama," Rosa said. "I've known some pretty nice white folks." Sylvester was still shaking his head when the first float bobbed beneath the river's surface.

"Easy!" Rosa said, but Sylvester had already pulled up on the cane. A brown bass flipped back and forth at the end of the string. It sparkled in the setting sun. "Good job," Rosa said. It wasn't as easy as he'd made it look, she knew. Pull too hard, and the hook yanks clear out of the fish's mouth. Pull too easy, and the fish just spits it out. "Swing it over here," she said. Rosa stepped on the fish to quiet it and twisted the hook free. She slipped another worm on and said, "Drop it right in."

Then she threaded the string in through the bass's gills and out its mouth. The driftwood stick meant it couldn't slip all the way through. "Good catch," Rosa held the string up. "Three or four more and we have us a fine dinner."

Sylvester grinned and swung the next hook into the water. Rosa caught the next one, then Sylvester landed another. The air was warm satin on their skin, and the first star just twinkling. They sat quiet by the river, watching the water flow past. "I guess three will do just fine." Rosa finally said. As they left, a whippoorwill began singing his name on the bank behind them. Sylvester whistled along with him for a while but then lost interest. *Nobody can keep up with that bird,* Rosa thought as they walked home. He'd be repeating his name, over and over, past supper, right through prayers, on into the darkness and through the night, every night, all summer long.

Sixty-seven Cents

Sylvester's legs swung beneath the table. Rosa knew how he felt, restless and ready to move. "Cotton's ready to pick," the word had come down from Moses Hudson. "All hands wanting a day's work, show at dawn tomorrow." The sky outside the window was already pale, and it looked to be a perfect fall morning.

"You sit still now, hear?" Grandma Rose turned to Sylvester. He straightened in his chair, and the old woman turned back to the Bible. "Listen close to this part, boy. You sure do need it."

Grandma Rose cleared her throat and read:

"'In quietness and in confidence shall be your strength.'" She paused, then said, "Amen."

Rosa silently repeated the verse to herself, then the reference: Isaiah 30:15. She promised herself to look it up in her Bible before bed, to see what followed this wonderful line.

Grandfather lifted his hands. "Dear Lord," he said, beginning the morning prayer. Around great-grandfather's table, the family bowed their heads. When the last "Amens" were said, they could finally leave.

The whole family stood together in the line of pickers at the edge of Moses Hudson's field. At the head of the line, Mr. Freeman handed out the cotton sacks, one by one. The field hands talked quietly, sharing bits of news. Some of it was about weddings and babies, but one was about the school. "Did y'all hear that the school over by Mount Zion is closed?" Rosa's heart fell. The black school was closed? Where would she study? She glanced at her mama. Education was so important to her. Surely she would think of a way to get her children to school. How often had she told them, "Education is the way out of the fields." What was she going to say now? But Mama was busy, talking to friends from church. Rosa knew better than to interrupt adults.

She looked out across Moses Hudson's land. Already a dozen neighbors were out in the field, picking the fluffy white bolls from the cotton plants. Only the full-grown men's sacks swung free from their shoulders. Everybody else's dragged along the ground behind them. None of the sacks were bulging yet, Rosa noticed. *It is still early,* she told herself.

She looked up into the sky and squinted. All the colors of dawn had melted into the clear warm blue of fall. There wasn't a cloud in sight to shade the pickers. Rosa glanced quickly at Grandma Rose. Grandfather did most of the complaining, but Rosa knew heat was hard on old women, too. Grandma was standing tall and proud, waiting for her sack.

"Your turn, Rosa." Mama gave her a gentle push from behind.

"Age?" Mr. Freeman asked. He didn't look up from his clipboard.

"Eleven, sir," she answered, and took a deep breath. She knew what was coming.

"Well, Rosa," Mr. Freeman said, adding her name to his list, "you be paid separate for all the cotton you pick today."

Rosa glanced back at her mama and grinned. Up to now, her pickings had been thrown in to the weighing along with Mama's and Sylvester's. This was the first time Rosa would know exactly how much she was earning for the family. Mrs. McCauley smiled back, and Rosa felt a thrill of pride.

"Time's a-wasting, girl," Mr. Freeman scolded. Rosa turned quickly and took the rough fabric sack he had been offering. "Start there, on the tenth row from the end." Rosa pulled the handle over her shoulder and hurried out of Mr. Freeman's way, her face burning with embarrassment. This was her first day in the fields on her own, and she'd held up the whole line. What a way to start the day!

Rosa rushed across the field toward where Mr. Freeman had pointed his pencil. Her old flour sack felt so light it floated behind her over the sandy red soil. The day was still cool. Meadowlarks sang from the fence posts along the edge of the field. *Eight,* Rosa counted the rows silently. *Nine, Ten.* She looked down her very own row. It stretched ahead, each withered cotton plant full of fluffy seed pods. *I'll fill this old sack in no time,* she promised herself, *if I just work right along.* Rosa reached for the first puffy boll as Mama took her place in the next row.

Rosa grabbed and twisted to break the pod free. It didn't want to come, so she tugged, and it popped off. Rosa tossed it into the yawning opening of her sack. The puff looked very little in there alone. Suddenly filling the whole bag seemed impossible. It would take years. Rosa looked down the row. It went on forever. Rosa sighed.

"That's how it always feels on the first day, Rosa," Mama said. "Remember?" Mrs. McCauley had not turned to look at her daughter, and her hands had not paused in their quick movements.

She used both of them at once, reaching deftly for two bolls, twisting and dropping them into the sack together. Then, smoothly, she reached out again. Rosa glanced into her Mama's bag. It was already beginning to fill out.

As Rosa grabbed the nearest cotton bolls in her row, she remembered, like her mother had told her to. The year she was six she had barely been able to see over the cotton plants. That first day she had been crying by supper break. *Had she been stung by a bee?* She tried to recall why she was so upset. *Was it breathless hot that day? Was there lightning?* She searched her mind for the memory and finally decided she'd just been bored by the endless work. *And tired.* She'd even taken a nap through the heat of the day. Rosa smiled at the mental picture of herself curled up between the rows, sleeping the afternoon away.

She shook her head to clear the memory, glanced into her bag, and blinked. There was more cotton in there than she'd expected. "You're right, Mama," she called. "Picking memories is a good way to pick a row."

"So is reviewing your Bible verses, Honey child," Mama called back to her. She was well ahead of her on the row. "Did you learn this morning's?"

Rosa thought quickly, "'In quietness and confidence shall be your strength,'" she called, trying to move her hands fast enough to keep up with her mother.

"Amen!" Mrs. McCauley's voice was warm.

"Now do your psalms," Grandmother Rose called across the rows. Rosa glanced at her and grinned. From her grandmother that was quite a challenge. Rosa had watched the old woman in church. Her lips moved along with every Bible verse the pastor ever read aloud. Rosa began with her favorite psalm, the twenty-third. Then she recalled the words of the one hundredth psalm. It was so short, and so beautiful, that it was no challenge to remember. Then she silently recited the twenty-seventh. She'd reread the ones like this that spoke to her over and over. Her hands flew as she went on to review other psalms. Then she recited other verses from the New and Old Testament.

When she looked up, the sky was bright, and the sun high. Rosa wiggled her shoulders and stretched her back. Her sack was nearly a quarter full! She tried to imagine how much money she would earn today for the family. Seventy-five cents? A whole dollar? She knew some of the best pickers could bring in over a dollar and a half a day. *Get moving,* she scolded herself.

Rosa urged her arms to reach faster, her hands to twist quicker, her fingers to hurl the bolls into the yawning cotton sack. Sweat rolled down her forehead. She licked her lips and pushed harder down the row. The afternoon became a blur. Pick and pick faster. She lost track of how many times she'd had to wipe her face, how many times she'd hushed the hunger growling in her stomach.

"Rosa."

It took a moment for Rosa to focus. Someone was calling her name. It was Mama.

"Time to break for a drink and a mite to eat."

Rosa stood straight and felt her back cramp. "Ouch!" She tried to keep her voice quiet. How could she complain, when Grandma Rose never said a word about her aches and pains? Rosa's arms were shaking with exhaustion, but she'd almost caught up with Mama.

"Rosa? You been picking in your sleep?" It was Mr. Freeman, on his horse. He took off his big hat and wiped his face with his arm.

Rosa looked back. She had been making good time, it was true, but she'd missed bolls here and there, and a good many lay on the ground where her wild tosses had missed the sack. While the others gathered in the shade of a tree, Rosa forced herself to go back and gather the missed bolls. Now the bag felt very heavy, dragging along the ground behind her. Its strap dug into her shoulder. By the time she caught up with her family, there was just time to gulp some water, gobble some biscuits, and gulp again to wash down the crumbs.

"You'd best set yourself a slower pace," Grandma Rose said. "'In returning and rest shall ye be saved.'"

That was from the morning's devotion, Rosa

thought with a start. The sun burned into her shoulders through the thin fabric of her dress. The hard, sandy soil baked the soles of her feet. Her back ached and her hands hurt. Rosa looked up at the sun and sighed. There were still hours of picking before sunset. How would she ever find the strength?

"In quietness and confidence," the answer came to her from the Bible. It was the rest of the verse that Grandma Rose had given her. Rosa thought about confidence first. *I can do this,* she told herself. *I've worked long days like this all my life.* She took a deep breath and began picking again. Her muscles still hurt, but the stiffness eased as she moved.

The quietness part was easy, too. She hadn't complained yet, and she wasn't about to start. Now that thought made her feel proud, and with the pride came a surge of energy. She listened to the quiet in the field. The breeze had died, and even the birds had hushed their songs. The pickers, scattered about the field, worked in silence. *They're all tired,* Rosa realized. *It's not just me!*

Then one of the men on the far side of the field began to sing. It was old song, a spiritual. "I am bound for the Promised Land . . . ," he sang. Mama joined in, then Grandma Rose. "Oh, who will come and go with me?" Soon the whole field was singing ". . . I am bound for the Promised Land." Rosa sang along quietly and realized that her hands were moving smoothly with the rhythm of the hymn.

She began thinking about the words as she sung them and felt strengthened. Her great-grandfather had probably sung this very song in the fields, she realized. She watched her hands, plucking, tossing, and swinging back to pluck again. *Great-grandfather's hands had moved to the same beat,* she thought. *He'd sung these words, thought these thoughts.*

When the last verse, and the "Amens" had died down, the field seemed very quiet. It wasn't an exhausted silence like before, Rosa thought. It was peaceful. Now Grandma Rose started another song. After the pickers had sung it through, someone from over by the road began another. One after another, they sang Rosa's favorites and spirituals she only barely remembered. The singing went through the long afternoon. When Mr. Freeman called an end to the picking, Rosa was surprised at how her sack bulged. And she'd emptied it once, before supper!

At the weighing in, Mr. Freeman announced, "A dollar for every hundred pounds." Rosa felt her shoulders sag as she waited in line. She knew she hadn't picked anywhere near a hundred pounds.

Mama patted her back. "A good day's work," she said.

The overseer put Rosa's bags on the scale and called out, "Sixty-seven cents!" Mr. Freeman counted out the coins into her hand. Rosa squeezed the handful tight. This was the most she had ever made in one day!

"Bless you," Grandma Rose said, as Rosa gave her the money. "This will help, sure enough."

A robin was singing its evening song as they walked home. No one else had the energy left to start another song. They plodded in silence. After a time, Rosa fell into step beside her mother. "Mama?" she began, then stopped. How could she bring up her worry? Nobody had actually told her the school was closing. Rosa had just been listening in on someone else's conversation. Rosa decided to wait. Anyway, her mother could probably teach her some at home on the weekends.

"You sound troubled, child," Mrs. McCauley said. They walked on together a piece. A whippoorwill began singing his endless song. "You thinking about school?"

"Yes," Rosa answered. *How had Mama known?*

"I been thinking some on it, too," Mama said. Rosa held her breath. Mama had a plan. Rosa could hear it in her voice.

"I'll be teaching again this year in Spring Hill," Mama said. "I know there are empty benches there. It would be a long walk for you, but . . ."

"Oh, Mama!" Rosa cried, "I can walk that far for sure."

She slowed her pace for a moment so she was even with Grandma Rose. "I get another year of school!" Rosa took the old woman's arm. As they walked together, she thought about the next year. "And you know what, Grandma Rose?" she said in wonder, "I'll get to see my mama every day of the week!"

Rosa rushed up to give her mother a hug. Then she skipped all the way home in the twilight.

Whites Only

Rosa loved the sixth grade in Spring Hill. To teach there, Mrs. McCauley had to live in the little town by the school. Rosa and Sylvester stayed with their grandparents in Pine Level. They walked eight miles to school every morning then home again in the evening. Some days the walk felt very long, but Rosa couldn't wait to see what her mother would be teaching that day.

Mrs. McCauley didn't just teach reading and writing and numbers. She showed the girls how to sew and crochet and knit, too. She helped them with their needlework and explained how to care for sick people. Rosa knew she would use all of these skills in her life, so she listened carefully. When Mama saw the students getting restless, she led exercises outdoors. She did nature crafts, too, with free materials the students could collect. Once, they made corn shuck dolls. Another time, they wove baskets out of the long, soft needles that grew on the pine trees around the school. The days seemed to fly by, but the long walks to school made Rosa's tonsils get infected again.

"She should have an operation to take them out," a country doctor told Rosa's mother. "She'd never be sick like this again."

"Will you do it?"

"Yes," the doctor said, "but her heart's too weak to put her to sleep for the operation."

"You mean to tell me she'd have to be wide awake while you cut inside her throat?" Mama shook her head. "You'll not be doing that to my daughter!"

Rosa missed more school. Finally Mrs. McCauley paid a neighbor to drive them into Montgomery where her sister lived. A city doctor did the operation—and he put Rosa to sleep so she didn't feel a thing. Rosa was so sick afterward that she had to stay in the hospital for extra days. She couldn't see, her eyes swelled, and her throat wasn't healing well. When she got home, she missed even more school. Slowly she healed. When she felt well again, she put on weight. She began to grow. Without her tonsils, she was healthier than she had been all her life.

There was no high school in the Alabama countryside for black children. If Rosa wanted to go beyond sixth grade, she had to move to the nearest city, Montgomery. There was a free, public high school for blacks there, and the McCauleys had aunts and uncles in town they could live with. "We're moving," Mama told Rosa. "But there is more news, Rosa," she said. "I want you to get the best education you can. I'm going to pay for you to go to the Montgomery Industrial School for Girls."

"Oh, we just call it Miss White's," one girl told Rosa as they stood in front of the school the first day. The girl was black. Rosa looked around. All of the girls were colored. There had to be three hundred of them—more than all the people in her church back home. There were no boys lined up on the cement steps. Rosa looked up. The school building was red brick. It was three stories high, and every window had glass in it!

"Who is Miss White?" Rosa asked, still looking at the huge building.

"Miss White's our principal," the girls around Rosa told her. "She's wonderful! She is the bravest white lady I know."

Rosa's head jerked back to the girl who was speaking. "She's white?"

"Sure 'nuff." the girl said. "All of our teachers are."

"And they teach in a black school?" Rosa could not believe what she was hearing. "They're all from the North," Rosa was told. She nodded. All the white people who were ever nice to her had come from the North. "And," the girl went on, "you can't believe how nasty the people of Montgomery are to them."

"Miss White's house has been burned down two times already," another girl said. "The fine white people here want to drive her away."

"Why?" Rosa asked. This sounded like what the KKK did to blacks, not to white ladies who taught school. "Whatever did she do to them?"

"They're afraid she'll give us ideas," a tall girl said. "About equality. And equal rights. And integration."

"What's that?" Rosa asked.

"That's when a school is open to both black and white children," someone said. "Segregation is what we have now. Whites and coloreds are kept apart."

"And don't the whites get all the good parts!" One girl laughed a bitter laugh.

"Integration," Rosa said the new word and laughed aloud. "Who'd ever heard tell of such a foolish thing?" She couldn't even picture it. The bell rang and the girls filed in quietly.

At first Rosa's mother paid the school's fee. Later Rosa earned her own way, dusting and sweeping, emptying the wastebaskets, and washing the blackboards. Rosa, her mother, and Sylvester were living with Mrs. McCauley's sister and her three children in a house on the edge of the city. Rosa loved being around the little children, but she didn't like her walk downtown to Miss White's school. Everything she saw made her hate segregation more.

The white neighborhoods had big houses with fancy lawns and gardeners to keep them looking pretty. Blacks were not allowed to live there. Movie theaters had separate doors marked COLORED, doors that led to the back of the building or the balcony. Many of the stores she walked past were segregated, too, with signs saying NO COLOREDS posted in their windows. At first Rosa glared right in through the glass. But no matter how beautiful the dolls were in the window, or how nice the clothes, no matter how much she needed a haircut, or a Band-Aid, she could not go inside.

"You make your eyes look down, Rosa," she remembered her mother saying. "You don't make trouble." Rosa would sigh and walk on.

Rosa liked her teachers, though it was hard to

get used to having white women in the front of the classroom. They were nice, once you got used to how strange they sounded. "A Massachusetts accent," another fifth grader told her. Rosa had been put back again, since she had missed so many days of school with her tonsillitis. Miss White also thought that the poor country schools didn't teach as well as her "Industrial School." Rosa knew differently, and made up her mind to catch up as quickly as she could.

It was hot on one of her first days in the new school. Rosa hadn't noticed while she was in the building. The teachers had opened the windows, and the lessons were too interesting to notice the weather outside. Rosa was learning more than she ever had about history and arithmetic, but also about sewing and nursing sick folks. Some of her classmates wanted to become seamstresses. Other girls were planning to work taking care of sick, rich people.

Rosa only knew she loved children. It would be so grand if she could be a teacher like her mother! She would need to learn her schoolwork well enough to share it with young people—even if it was only for her own children. No matter what came in life, she knew that she would need the sewing, and if anyone in her family ever became ill, she would need the nursing, too. It all mattered, so Rosa listened closely to her teachers.

During recess, Miss White's girls played outside in a yard with a big fence on one side. On the other side of the fence, they could hear other children playing. Her classmates told her it was a Catholic school. Rosa wanted to meet a Catholic, until a few of them climbed up the fence. They hung over the edge and started yelling. It was just like being teased from the white school buses back in Pine Level.

Miss White hurried out and shooed the children off the fence. She told her girls that there was nothing wrong with being black. She reminded them that they had just as much dignity as any white person. It made Rosa feel better, especially hearing it from a white person as nice as Miss White.

By the end of that day, Rosa was tired. The heat hit her as she walked out of the building. It shimmered on the sidewalks and baked the roads. Passing trolley cars swept clouds of hot dust up from their rails.

Rosa wished it wasn't so far from school to Aunt Fannie's house. *It's not that far,* she scolded herself. *It's nothing like walking all those miles to Spring Hill School.* But the sidewalk was hotter than dirt. The exhaust coming from cars was hot, too, gray and choking. Rosa thought about breathing that sooty air into her lungs. It made her want a drink.

NO COLOREDS read a sign on a window she passed. It seemed to Rosa to be shouting right at her. She rushed past, swallowing the dust on her tongue. HELP WANTED—WHITES ONLY snarled another sign. Rosa hurried on through the heat. A white family was coming the other way, so she lowered her gaze and stepped off the sidewalk into the street.

The rich lady didn't say "Excuse me." Her fat little children didn't thank her either. *Did they even see me?* Rosa felt her lips tighten. *It's not fair.* The familiar thought began simmering in her mind. As she stepped back onto the sidewalk, she glanced up. Ahead she saw a water fountain at the end of the next block. Rosa was suddenly glad to be in the big city. Pine Level was too small to have water fountains. She promised herself a long, cool drink to wash away all the dust and hot anger.

Halfway down the block, Rosa stopped, right in the middle of the sidewalk. There was a sign over the fountain. It said, WHITES ONLY.

It can't be, Rosa argued silently. Her tongue felt dry in her mouth. She tried to swallow, but couldn't. What would happen if she drank this white water?

She didn't dare try it and see. There were racists back in Pine Level who handed out beatings whenever they were cross with a black. She stared at the hateful sign. She had to obey.

She broke into a run. Two blocks later, another fountain stood. It was crusted with rust and dirt. The sign on it said COLOREDS.

Rosa stopped and stared. There was no way she would drink from that fountain—or any other in this cruel, segregated city! She ran on, past businessmen, past barking dogs, through the white neighborhood. Her breaths were coming in hot gasps now. She ran up her aunt's front steps.

"Afternoon," she greeted her cousins, sitting on the porch.

"What's wrong?" one of them called. Rosa didn't stop to answer. She didn't pause until she was in the kitchen with a big glass of water in her hand. She drank it without taking a breath. *I'll never, never drink from any of their fountains,* she promised herself, and poured another glassful.

One by one, her cousins filed into the kitchen with her. "What's wrong, Rosa?" the oldest asked.

"Not a thing," Rosa knew she was telling a lie, but she hated to complain.

"You surely are thirsty," the littlest one said, watching Rosa finish the second glass of water.

Rosa smiled at her. "I ran home."

"Why, Rosa?" The little girl asked, "It be too hot to run."

Rosa looked at the floor. "I didn't want to drink at the fountains," she told her cousins. "Not the colored one. Not the white one either."

"You best not even think to touch those white fountains, girl," the oldest said. "It's against the law, and the police are mean clear through about it."

"They hit," the little girl explained.

"They hit you?" Rosa was horrified. She looked around at her cousins. "They can do that?"

"None of us have been pushed about by any police—or any whites. We be careful about those Jim Crow laws, the ones that keep coloreds and whites apart."

Segregation again. Rosa felt a chill. There weren't so many laws about this in Pine Level. Mostly out there, there weren't so many whites around. As far as she knew, the blacks just kept to themselves. But she remembered the nice old lady who'd taught her to fish, and Mr. Freeman who was in charge of Moses Hudson's fields. He was hard, but he was fair. Then there were the white children, like Franklin, who just made trouble to make himself feel big. *And,* the thought sent more chills down her back, *the night riders who came to attack.*

"Tell me," she said, quickly, "what should I know here so they don't get after me."

They teased her for being from the country, but then they got serious. "If a place doesn't say COLORED and you don't see some blacks inside, don't you go in there."

"You can go into a drugstore through the door that says COLORED, but don't you dare sit down and order food."

"What if I'm thirsty?" Rosa asked, "or I want a Coke and aspirin for a headache?" She thought a minute. "What if I want an ice cream?" Her cousins just shook their heads at her. "But I love ice cream," Rosa argued.

"You can't even use a bathroom, Rosa, unless it says COLORED."

"You always have to sit in the back of a trolley, too."

"What if the back seats are filled?" Rosa asked.

"You can sit in the middle section, until more

whites get on. Then you have to stand and let them have the seat."

"No!" Rosa was stunned by this rule. "You mean that old Grandma Rose would have to ride standing up just so a spoiled little white boy could sit?"

They explained that Grandma Rose and everybody else in that whole row of seats would have to stand, so the white boy didn't have to even sit with a colored person.

"You get on and pay at the front," the oldest one told her, "then you get off again and hurry to the back to get on. Run, 'cause sometimes the driver pulls away before you get back on."

Rosa felt sick to her stomach. *That's not fair!* she wanted to yell, but her cousins weren't done. "It's the Jim Crow laws, Rosa."

"Who is this Jim Crow?" Rosa grumbled. "I don't like him one little bit."

Her cousins laughed. It was a bitter sound. "It's not a who, Rosa." the little one said. "Least ways I don't think it's a real person. It's just laws."

"I heard it was a white singer man a hundred years ago," the middle cousin said. "He danced onstage with his face painted black, pretending to be colored."

"I don't know about that," the oldest said, "but if you break those Jim Crow laws, Rosa, the police come. You don't want that."

Rosa shook her head. She surely did not. She promised them she'd keep out of trouble. Couldn't the whites see how unfair all these laws were? A Bible verse came to her mind. "But many that are first shall be last, and the last shall be first." It gave her a bit of peace. It might not be until they went to the Promised Land, but there would be justice someday. God said so, right in the Bible.

Rosa often walked to school with her cousins. They didn't go all the way to Miss White's, but it was fun to walk with them as far as the public school. As Rosa hurried on alone after that, she often thought about what fun it was to be with the little children.

One morning, before the cousins got to their school, a white boy was swooping along the sidewalk toward them on roller skates. They all moved out of the way as he came closer. Suddenly he looked straight at Rosa. Her heart fell. His face had the same mean look that Franklin's had. This boy was going to do something to her. And Rosa couldn't do anything at all back. *It's not fair!* the words were echoing in her mind as the boy skated right into her, bumping her off the sidewalk.

Rosa didn't stop to think. She lunged back at him and pushed him off balance.

"Stop that nigger! She's attacking my son!" a woman standing nearby shrieked.

Rosa turned in wonder. "But he pushed me first," she said. *Don't talk back!* she told herself, but it was too late.

"I saw it, girl. It was, too, your fault," the woman hissed. "And I can get you put so far in jail for it, you'll never get out again."

Rosa swallowed hard. Then she swallowed again. *"In quietness and confidence,"* she reminded

97

herself. She looked down and forced herself to mumble an apology.

"Oh, my dear, dear little honey child!" The woman had pushed by her and was patting her son. "Are we hurt? Do we have a scratch on that little knee?" she crooned. There was clearly no scratch on him anywhere. She glared over her shoulder at Rosa then back to her son. "See? What has Mommy always told you? We just can't trust their kind." The boy sniffled a loud, fake sniff. "Would ice cream make it all better?" she offered, and led him into the drugstore.

Rosa's cousins gathered around her. Their silence scolded her as they walked on toward school. Rosa tried not to think about her own scraped knee and the sticky blood soaking into her stocking. Her knee didn't matter. She could have been in jail.

That evening at supper, as the cousins told Aunt Fannie about the white mother's threat, Mrs. McCauley got very quiet. Within days, Rosa's mother announced that they were moving.

She didn't want her daughter to be walking through the white neighborhood to get to school every day. It wasn't safe. Rosa had to say good-bye to all of her little cousins and go with Sylvester and Mama to live at an older cousin's home, nearer to Miss White's school.

Setting Rosa's Sights

The Montgomery Industrial School for Girls closed after a year and a half. Miss White was old. She had struggled for years to keep a school for African-American girls open in the segregated South. It meant she was not welcome in Montgomery's white churches, invited into the homes of whites, or welcome in their clubs or at parties. They called her a "Yankee nigger lover"—and worse. She was finally ready to give up and move back to Massachusetts.

Teenage Rosa was sad to leave the school, but she had learned lessons there that would last all her life. "No drinking, no dancing, and no movies. No dating. Sunday manners every day. Dress like a lady." There was no end to the strict rules at Miss White's. Rosa knew the rules and knew that she followed them. That confidence gave Rosa dignity and self-respect. Now she knew exactly how a young lady—black or otherwise—should act. Most important, Miss White had taught her that she should not set her sights lower than anybody else's just because she was black.

It was a message she had always heard from her own mother and from Grandma Rose. It was repeated in ninth grade at a new public school in Montgomery, the Booker T. Washington Junior High School. Rosa and her family moved back in with Aunt Fannie that year. Her aunt was living in a black neighborhood now, where Mrs. McCauley felt her children would be safe.

Aunt Fannie was getting older. She was very

thin and growing weak. It was hard for her to finish all of her work at the Jewish country club where she was a cleaning lady. Rosa's mama was suffering from migraines, so she had her hands full keeping her own job. Running the house and feeding all of those children cost a lot. Often, Rosa and the younger cousins went to the county club with her aunt to help out after school and in the summer. The little ones loved Rosa. She was patient and good and always ready to talk to them.

"That white boy said something awful to me!" a cousin might say.

Rosa would hug her and answer, "All he did was mouth off at you? Honey, if that's all it was, you'd best forget about it."

Rosa had become quick to forgive white kids who teased blacks. "He just didn't know any better," she explained. "Sounds crazy, but his mama and daddy must have taught him to talk like that."

Rosa did not forgive the parents as easily.

° ° °

In tenth grade Rosa switched schools again. Now she attended the laboratory school, which was at Montgomery State Teachers College. While young college women were being trained to be teachers, they could practice on Rosa and the other high school students.

Rosa wanted to finish high school, and she was almost there. By now education meant as much to her as it did to her mother. In the 1920s, few blacks in the South ever graduated. In smaller towns, like Pine Level, there often was no school at all. Even when there was a school, many pupils had to drop out to take jobs to help their parents. Other students started their own families and had to spend all their time earning money to support themselves.

"If you graduate," the teachers told her, "you can expect more money in your paychecks for the rest of your life." Her mother had told her over and over that "a diploma means you don't have to work in the fields or as a cleaning lady." Most good-paying jobs required a high school diploma. It meant security. It meant dignity.

Rosa knew how people respected her own mother for being a teacher.

Sixteen-year-old Rosa began eleventh grade determined to finish school. She was still studying at the laboratory school, seeing college students every day. A hope began to grow in her heart.

One night after supper, Aunt Fannie read a letter from Grandma Rose. She looked up at Rosa with tears in her eyes. "Your grandmother is sick," she said.

Rosa did not have to ask how sick she was. She could see it in her aunt's eyes. The next day in school, Rosa had trouble listening in her classes. While the teacher was talking about algebra, Rosa was thinking of how often Grandma Rose had nursed her through tonsillitis. No matter how tired the old woman was, or how hot the kitchen was, Grandma had always made special soups for her. She had sat by her bedside, feeding her, spoonful by spoonful. She had done Rosa's farm chores when Rosa was too weak.

And no matter how late Grandma Rose had

stayed up, holding Rosa's hand, she was always ready the next morning at great-grandfather's table with a Bible devotion to give them all strength.

A bell rang, surprising Rosa out of her memories. Around her, classmates were gathering their books. Rosa moved like a robot, walking to her next class. She didn't hear her friends' greetings, or the English teacher's first assignment.

"Rosa, will you kindly join our class?" the teacher teased. Rosa was a good student, and her teachers respected her. Normally she would have smiled back, but Rosa's face felt too numb to move. Who was feeding the chickens back at the farm? Who was canning the okra, drying the beans, and picking the last of the fall harvest? Rosa had watched Grandma Rose stoke the stove until the fire was high then haul hot iron kettles of preserves and jams from there to the table. The old woman couldn't be doing that now that she was sick.

The nuts needed to be gathered. Biscuits had to be made every morning before breakfast. The floors needed to be swept; the cow milked twice a day. The Mount Zion Church people would help, of course, but they couldn't move right in to the little farmhouse. Could Mama go back home to take on the work?

Rosa shook her head, then looked around the room, embarrassed. No one in her class had noticed. That was fine with Rosa. She didn't want to complain to anyone. And she didn't need a classmate to tell her that Mama was not the answer. Her mother was not well, either. Mrs. McCauley's migraine headaches were so bad that she had to stay in bed some days. And when she could get to work, her legs and ankles swelled up, and it was hard for her to walk. Mama couldn't take on Grandma Rose's chores, too. It was enough for her to take care of herself just now. Who could help Grandma Rose?

By the end of the class, Rosa still hadn't come up with any answer—except the one she didn't even want to think about.

But Rosa had to think about it. Her next class was domestic science. This fall's unit was home care of the elderly. Rosa kept picturing her grandmother sick, and home at the farm. The teacher was talking about special care for people too sick to get out of bed anymore. "Lying in one position for days," she explained, "can cause bedsores. If the patient is too weak to turn themselves over, someone else has to turn them. The sores have to be washed and dried carefully."

Someone in the back of the room groaned at the idea. A few other students giggled. The teacher looked at them sharply. "If you don't take care of bedsores," she scolded, "they get infected." Rosa felt like the teacher was talking just to her. "Bedsores hurt something terrible, and the infection can spread and kill a patient." No one in the room was laughing now. As the teacher showed the students how to roll a patient over without hurting their old, stiff joints, Rosa blinked back tears.

What if Grandma Rose needed this kind of help, and no one was there?

Hospitals in the South would not treat African-American people. Most doctors would not bother with them either. It was up to a black's family and friends to get them through illnesses.

The rest of the day was a blur for Rosa. Her body moved through school and walked home. She went to her after-school job and washed all of a white lady's windows without thinking once about what she was doing. Her mind was wild with worry. *Grandma Rose needs me. Now. There isn't anybody else.* Guilt and love washed over her. *I should just quit school and go home.* She had finally thought the dreadful answer. It was the right thing to do—and Rosa knew it. *But I can't quit school now! Not this close to graduating!*

Rosa wanted to yell, to scream, to cry. Mama had wanted so much for her to finish school. It was Rosa's dream, too. And that dream was crumbling. Complaining never helped anything, she knew. She kept her feelings to herself.

Rosa finished up at work, said her good-byes politely, and went home. Over the next weeks, she read her Bible for guidance and waited for word of Grandma Rose's condition. Rosa's body was still going to school, but now her mind was back at the farm. By the end of the month, she had moved back home to take care of Grandma Rose.

It was a gift to be able to ease the old woman's suffering. Rosa used everything she had learned about nursing in school. She remembered all of the kind things Grandma Rose had done when her tonsils were infected. She did the farm chores, too, and, at the end, she sat by the bedside, read the Bible aloud, and prayed with her grandmother.

Grandma Rose died about a month after Rosa went home to help her.

The death left Rosa in a fog of sorrow. She made herself go back to Montgomery. She asked State Teachers College if she could return to their laboratory school. The teachers said yes. They knew how much it meant to her.

Rosa heard that a factory was looking for seamstresses to sew denim work shirts every afternoon. Rosa loved sewing, and they were hiring colored people for the job. It was 1929, and the country was in a depression. Jobs were

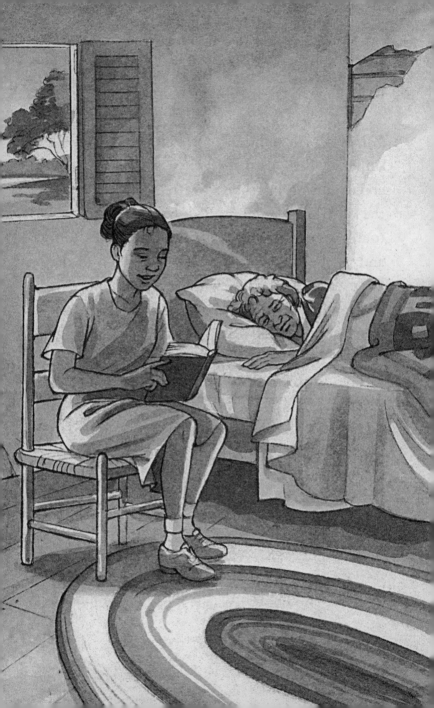

very scarce, and Rosa was glad to take this one. It felt good to have her life back on track—with a real job and a diploma just a few months away. She worked hard at school and at the factory. The work—and her faith—began to heal the hole left by her grandmother's death.

But soon Mama's illnesses got worse. Most days her feet were so swollen that she couldn't stand up at all. Rosa's mother couldn't hold a job. She needed someone to take care of her. Once again, Rosa faced a terrible decision.

She could decide to quit school and take care of her mother. Rosa's job paid well. It would pay more if she could spend more hours at the factory. She enjoyed nursing. It had made her feel good to make her grandmother's last weeks more comfortable.

Or she could decide to stay in school and try to finish. It wouldn't be easy now. Rosa had fallen far behind. Since she worked so many hours, she had missed a lot of classes. She had spent a whole month away from school when Grandma

Rose was dying. The choice was easier this time.

Once again, she quit school. This time she knew it was for good. *Someday,* she promised herself, *someday I'll get that diploma.* But she didn't really believe it.

Rosa just felt very lucky to have a job as the country's depression got worse. Most people had no work at all. Men stood in long lines waiting for handouts of bread to give their families. Some lived on the pennies they could get selling apples. Homeless people, called hobos, wandered the country, searching for any work that would pay them. Since they had no money, they couldn't buy train tickets. Instead, they waited beside the train tracks and hopped onto a train when it slowed down. These hobos jumped off when they came to another town. They might beg for food there or work a few hours for pennies before hopping back on a train again. Times were bad.

The church was Rosa's happiness. She belonged to the Saint Paul AME Church in Montgomery now. There was laughter there and singing. The church members helped each other. The ceremonies were long and joyful. And the pastor's sermons helped to make her faith rock solid. Besides Sunday services, the church had Bible meetings midweek and prayer meetings, too. Sister Rosa went to all of them. "'Thy faith has saved thee,'" it said in the Bible, "'go in peace.'" And Rosa did.

She sewed shirts at the factory. Other times, she worked cleaning people's houses, cooking, or doing their laundry. She took in sewing projects for people who needed to have a dress made larger or smaller or pants shortened. She even sold fruit at street fairs—anything to make a living.

Rosa paid little attention to the news or politics. Things were changing in the South. The depression was getting worse and everyone was trying to get the same few jobs. The stress made angry people even angrier about everything—including race. Black men who had served in the army in World War I had come home changed. While they could only fight in units with other colored soldiers, they had traveled far beyond the American South. They had gotten to know black soldiers from the North, where there were no Jim Crow segregation laws. The men had seen how much better the rest of the world treated blacks. Some of them had been leaders in their own units. They all came home expecting to be treated differently.

White people were also angry. Not only were the African Americans taking away scarce jobs, they were getting "uppity." They wouldn't just put their eyes down and get out of the way anymore. They expected better treatment. Some even talked about integration, like they had seen in the North. The Ku Klux Klan and other racist terrorists attacked more often, trying to keep blacks "in their place." Hangings and beatings, burnings and whippings, Klansmen would do anything under the cover of their cowardly robes.

Teenage Rosa lived quietly with her mother, and they were careful, so she was never attacked. She had her church friends and friends at work. She dated sometimes, but none of the men were special in her life. Jazz was the glorious new music, but Rosa still didn't dance. Women were wearing more makeup, but Rosa refused to paint her face. She was still following all the rules Miss White had taught her. She did not drink, smoke, or go to the movies. Her life had a dreary pattern to it, splashed only with the joy and excitement of her Christian worship. It was almost enough, but Rosa was ready for a change.

Danger

"I have somebody I'd like you to meet," one of Rosa's friends said one day. "He's quite a nice gentleman and he's lonely. He just broke up with his old girlfriend."

When eighteen-year-old Rosa laughed and said no, her friend pointed him out. "That's him. Raymond Parks. We all just call him Parks."

Now Rosa knew she was not interested. She knew who Parks was. He was one of those young men active in a new club, the National Association for the Advancement of Colored People. This NAACP group met in a church.

That sounded safe, but they were trying to get fair treatment for blacks. They wanted people of color to be able to go into the Montgomery Public LIbrary, use the city parks, and have rights equal to a white citizen's. It was dangerous to be part of a group like that. The Ku Klux Klan often picked on blacks who were willing to lead in their community. When these new leaders started to speak out about equal rights, the KKK made sure somebody beat them up.

It was no protection to be living in Montgomery, the capital of the whole state of Alabama. The beatings happened in the shadow of the huge, white marble Capitol Building, high up on its hill. A big bronze star stood on its front porch. It marked where Jefferson Davis had sworn to be a faithful president of the Confederate States of America. Confederate flags flew all about, reminding everyone that Southerners had fought bravely to keep their slave-owning way of life.

It was clear that nobody in this Alabama government would help the blacks. In fact, many of them supported the Klan. Even the governor of

Alabama was a proud KKK member. Many others joined them in secretly believing that whites were God's supreme race. White supremacists thought that everybody else—blacks, Orientals, Latinos, Jews, Catholics—was worthless. This idea made it easy for them to do brutal things to other human beings.

Blacks tried not to be noticed by these vicious bullies. Rosa knew that, and she had been careful to lead a quiet, good life. Being seen with an activist like Raymond meant danger. Dating him would be worse. It wasn't worth the risk, she felt. Besides, they probably couldn't change anything anyway. Rosa even told her friend that she liked men with far darker skin than Raymond's to get her to stop matchmaking.

But her friend kept nagging. Finally Rosa gave in. They met and talked. Raymond Parks asked, "May I come calling on you at your home?"

"No, please," Rosa said. She didn't want people to think she was dating him.

Parks didn't give up. He went looking for her

in Montgomery. When he found her house, Mrs. McCauley was out on the porch. She invited him in, and Rosa had to talk to him. She was not impressed.

The next time he came by, she wouldn't even leave her bedroom to speak to him. "I'm not going to give up," Rosa heard him tell Mama out on the porch.

"Come on, Rosa," he pleaded another day. "Just come out for a drive with me this afternoon." Rosa was impressed with Park's little red sportscar. She knew he was in his late twenties and had a good job as a barber, but few blacks owned their own cars in 1931. As Parks drove through the summer sunshine, he told her about his life. He'd been born in February, too, almost exactly ten years before Rosa, out in the country near Montgomery. It turned out that they had a lot more in common.

"Daddy left my mama when I was just a little one," he told her.

"Mine, too," Rosa said.

"I was the only black in an all-white

neighborhood, and no one would play with me," Parks said.

Rosa looked at the handsome young man beside her. Parks could have passed for white, except for the beautiful, tight kinkiness of his hair. "My brother, Sylvester, took a lot of teasing about his pale skin," she told him.

"They never let us forget that we're colored," he said. "I couldn't go to their white school. My mama taught me to read and write at home."

"Mine, too," Rosa said. "But you mean to tell me you never went to school?"

"A few months, here and there. Mostly I been taking care of my mama and my grandma." Rosa stared at him. It was like he was telling her story instead of his. "Grandma died when I was a teenager," he said, his voice breaking.

"Oh, Parks, I am sorry." Rosa put her hand on his arm. "I know how that feels."

"Mama died, too," he said, looking out of the car's window. "I've been on my own since then."

Rosa could hardly believe that this gentle man had led such a hard life. Parks was so smart. He read a lot, teaching himself about the world and its great thinkers. He could talk about ancient history or today's news. Education was important to Parks, even though he was self-educated. "Rosa," he told her, "you should go ahead and get that high school diploma." Parks was also the first man Rosa had ever spoken to who was willing to talk about race.

"I stand up to whites when they give me trouble," he said. "They know they're no better than me." It sounded dangerous to Rosa, but Parks told her, "If you act afraid, they'll just be harder on you." Rosa liked the fact that he wasn't meek.

He told her that he was working to help free the Scottsboro Boys. Rosa knew all about them. Everybody did. Back in March, nine black teenagers had jumped on a train, and were riding overnight in a car together. They were from all over Alabama and had just met. They'd spent hours sleeping and talking and laughing, swapping stories, and sharing their hopes for a job somewhere down the railroad line. There were other hobos on the train, too, white and black.

121

There were even a few women. At one point, some of the whites turned ugly, throwing gravel at the teenagers, threatening them.

The boys fought back and drove their attackers off the train at the next stop. When the train stopped in Scottsboro, Alabama, an angry mob of whites was waiting for them, waving sticks and guns. "Hang them!" they shouted. "Kill the niggers!" They claimed the boys had beaten up a couple of white hobos and thrown them from the train.

"They attacked me, too," one woman decided to claim. "They hurt me bad!" Another woman said, "They used sticks and knives on me and waved guns!" She wasn't bruised or bleeding, but the crowd wanted the excitement of lynching someone. The ropes were strung and the nooses knotted.

"We didn't do nothin'!" the youngest, a twelve-year-old boy, cried.

"Don't kill us!" the oldest boy, eighteen years old, pleaded. It didn't make any difference.

Just in time, the police came along. "You're all

under arrest," they said. The sheriff stopped the mob by promising a quick trial. They put the boys in handcuffs and took them to the nearest jail to wait. That saved the boys' lives—but only for a while.

"That's the one!" one of the women said the next day. "And him, and him, too. They attacked me." It made no sense, but the police decided the others had probably battered her, too. They charged all of the teens with assault and rape.

A trial was arranged. A jury was chosen in a hurry—and it was all white men. Some black ministers from Tennessee raised fifty dollars to hire a country lawyer to help the boys in court. He could only meet with the boys for a half an hour before the trial.

"Your Honor, they threatened me with guns, and cut me with knives, and beat me, too," the woman told the judge. "I just couldn't protect myself."

The jury heard that no guns or knives were ever found. They heard a doctor say that he had found no knife wounds or bruises on the women.

They heard each and every boy swear he was innocent.

But the jury didn't care. "Guilty!" they said. "They're all guilty."

The judge banged his gavel and said, "For all of you boys, except the twelve year old here, the sentence is death."

It was April 9. The Scottsboro Boys were taken in chains to jail. There they waited for July 10 to take their turns dying in the electric chair.

The newspapers around the country were full of the story. Even in the South, most people were horrified by the injustice. White supremacists were thrilled. The KKK celebrated. The police and the courts would not back down.

"I'll never sleep well until they're free," Parks stormed, his dark eyes flashing. The car was full of his anger—and his excitement. "Some of us are raising money to pay for a new lawyer for the boys," he told Rosa. "They have to get a new trial!"

It was worse than Rosa had imagined. Parks

wasn't just angry about this, he was doing something to change things. She wouldn't think what the KKK would do to him if they found out. This Raymond Parks was so brave!

"You remind me of my grandfather," she told him. "He was full of fire and courage."

"He protected me," she went on. "Back when I was four, the KKK started riding back and forth on the main road every night, right past our house. I listened through the window to the gravel crunching under their boots and their laughter." Rosa paused, remembering the sounds. Night after night, the Klansmen picked a house to attack. Sometimes neighbors were beaten. Sometimes they only burned a cross on the yard to scare everyone. A few blacks had been lynched, hung right by their houses.

"You don't have to tell me the kinds of things they were doing," Parks said gently. "I know."

"I was so afraid to go to sleep," she remembered, and shivered at the memory. "But you should have seen Grandfather!" she went on. "He was so brave. Every night he sat by the front door with his old, double-barreled shotgun across his knees. 'Don't you worry one little bit,' he told us. 'I'm sure to get the first one who comes through the door.'" She could still hear the fierce sound of his voice.

"You don't have to go on," Parks said.

"No," Rosa sighed, "I do. It is good to talk about it at last. I've never told anyone how I curled up on the carpet by his feet, waiting. Half the time, I fell asleep there." Rosa crossed her arms and hugged herself in the dark of the car. "Parks, I wanted to see him use that gun."

Raymond waited for a few moments of silence, then asked, "What happened?"

"I prayed every night. I heard those men outside, and I cried and I prayed to God to keep us safe, to make the Klan go away and leave us be." Rosa paused. "And you know what, Parks?"

"What, Rosa, Honey?"

"God answered my prayers."

"Praise the Lord," Parks echoed her thoughts.

Rosa sat silent in the dark car. Raymond had listened to her story—and she knew he understood the mix of terror and anger, helplessness and frustration. It felt good to talk about it all. It made it seem real, too, instead of just a memory she was trying to forget. But hearing it aloud made it seem even worse. Rosa could feel her old anger coming back. *It really* isn't *fair,* she thought. She knew Parks felt the same way—but that he was working to change things.

When Parks asked her to go riding again, she said yes.

On their second date, Raymond began talking about marriage. Rosa didn't quite say yes, but she didn't quite say no either. Parks must have figured it sounded good to her. The next day, when Rosa was away at church, he asked Mrs. McCauley, "May I marry your daughter?"

Mama said, "Yes."

When Rosa got home, her mother told her she was engaged.

Rosa and Raymond Parks were married a few months later, in December of 1931, at Rosa's home in Pine Level. It wasn't as happy an event as it could have been. Everyone missed Grandma Rose. It was a very quiet ceremony, with only a few family members invited.

There was no money for a honeymoon, so the couple went back to Montgomery to live in a small house on a quiet road in a black neighborhood. They were near the State Teachers College, where Rosa had gone to the laboratory school. Soon after they were married, Rosa began studying again to get her high school diploma.

Parks went back to work during the day in his barbershop. During the night, he had meetings. Sometimes it was the NAACP. Rosa was proud to hear about how the group was working to change the rules so that blacks could get treatment at Montgomery's public hospitals. Every other week, he met with the National Committee to Defend the Scottsboro Boys. He didn't always tell Rosa what the meetings were or what they were about. He wouldn't even tell her who was involved. "I tell you what," he told her the first time she asked, "I'm just going to call them all Larry. The less you know, the better. That way, if the police ask you, you really can't give them any secrets."

The first time a meeting was held at her house, Rosa got a good look at the table full of guns and the circle of men called "Larry" seated around it. She ran out onto the porch and crumpled down on the top step. She buried her head in her arms and froze there, stunned. Now she really knew how dangerous it all was. This was her future with Parks, courage and action, danger and love.

Somewhere in the shadows by the street, a man coughed. Rosa's head jerked up. She could just see the glint of the dim porchlight on the gun of another "Larry" standing guard over the house.

If any Ku Klux Klansman—or any other white extremist—found out they were meeting there, the men would need all of those guns. Rosa knew they were ready to use them. She had seen their faces. They all looked as fierce as her grandfather's had. As fierce as Parks swearing that he'd never sleep until the boys were freed.

Rosa closed her eyes and buried her face again. She needed to be alone with her thoughts. Things weren't fair. She knew that. Complaining wouldn't make any difference. Being sweet and quiet and making your eyes look down all your life wasn't the way either. Brave people like Parks and all the Larrys had to act. They had to fight to make things better. This was the only way things would ever change.

Rosa knew they were risking their lives. Now her life was in danger, too. But surely all the anger and fire she'd seen in those faces could make a difference. She prayed for quiet. For confidence. For strength. For safety. The night air wrapped her in a warm, soft blanket.

Hours later, she heard footsteps sneaking away through the bushes. Others shuffled through the house then tiptoed off down the street. Rosa

didn't move. The porch floor creaked and the step beneath her sagged. She felt the warmth of Park's body sitting next to her. His strong arm wrapped around her shoulders. "You can come in now," he said. "The meeting is over."

Rosa still couldn't move. Parks sat long into the night, quietly talking to her. He told her that he would never let her come to these meetings. It was too dangerous. "You couldn't run fast enough to get away," he told her. "They'd get you." He shifted on the hard wooden step. "And they'd get me too—because I would never leave you behind."

Rosa knew what he meant. What Parks was doing, only he could do. She would have to find some other way to help. Someday she would hear the call, and then she would act. God would protect her until then.

The best she could do now was to finish her education. She put her energy into study and work. In 1933, at twenty-one, Rosa finally got her high school diploma. Raymond was in the audience, clapping.

Fighting to Vote

"Be careful." Rosa must have said that to Parks a thousand times. She loved him. She was proud of the work he was doing. But every time he was out of her sight, she worried. Now she had more reason than ever.

"There's good news about the Scottsboro Boys!" he told her one day. "The Supreme Court of the United States heard all about their fake trial in Scottsboro. They told the town that the boys have to get a whole, new trial. A fair one!" Rosa clapped her hands in joy. "There's more," Parks said. "They got the money for a big-time lawyer, too!"

"Now where'd those poor black boys get that kind of money from?" Rosa asked.

"Some people calling themselves the International Labor Defense (ILD) just gave it to them. I hear they're a Communist group, but they have the money the boys need."

"Oh, Parks," Rosa shook her head, "now the racists are going to hate you twice as much. They're going to think you are a Communist as well as a black activist."

"It gets worse," Parks told her. "The lawyer they hired is Jewish. You know how these white supremacists think."

He was right. The Scottsboro lawyer snarled that "Alabama justice cannot be bought and sold with Jew money from New York." They needed that money, though, plus all the rest that Parks and the NAACP could collect. Racists were angry at being forced to do the trial over again—and especially furious because they might lose when everyone in the world was looking.

Tempers flared. Blacks all over the South were beaten for no reason, then arrested and charged with being "Communists." Two of the "Larry" men who met with Parks were shot dead. One night, soon after his friends died, Parks went out to another meeting.

"Be careful," Rosa whispered to him from the porch swing.

"Where's Raymond going this evening?" her landlord asked.

Parks looked at her sharply. Rosa swallowed hard and lied. "Oh, just out to a church meeting." She turned to Raymond. "You mind what I said," she told him.

Raymond smiled at her and disappeared around some bushes and into the night.

Suddenly, a pair of policemen came roaring by on motorcycles. Rosa jumped and fought to keep the swing moving smoothly. It wouldn't do to have her landlord—and the police—know how worried she was. The motorcycles turned around at the end of the narrow city street and came back again. They were driving slowly now. Rosa froze. The porch swing beneath her stopped as still as the night air. She couldn't see the faces of the men on their motorcycles, but she knew they were white. African Americans were never hired as police in Montgomery.

The landlord kept talking to her. He nodded toward the police, then winked at Rosa—and he just kept talking. Crickets chirped and night hawks buzzed in the sky over them, but there was nothing else normal about this night.

Hours went by. The police were still waiting. It was clear they were watching for Raymond to come home. What would they do to him then? Rosa could barely breathe—but she could pray.

Suddenly she heard her husband's familiar footsteps in the dark house behind her. Parks was safe! He had snuck through the bushes and come in silently through the back door. Rosa wanted to shout his name, run inside, and hug him. Instead, she made herself sit still awhile longer. Then she yawned and stretched right out on the porch where anyone could see her. The landlord politely looked away. "Good night," she told him, louder than she needed to, then, "God bless." And she went into the house. The police never knew Parks was home. She had fooled them!

She hadn't fooled her landlord. "I knew just how scared you were," he told her later. "That old porch swing was rattling and trembling along with every shiver of fear in your body."

"Mama," Rosa said, "I don't know how much longer I can keep this up."

"You can do anything with God's help," Mrs. McCauley scolded her.

"Sometimes I don't feel helped very much," Rosa admitted. "Things are really bad."

"You still reading your Bible every day, child?" Mama asked sharply. Rosa hung her head. She felt like a little girl again, ready for a scolding she knew she needed. "Why, Rosa Louise McCauley Parks," Mama said, her voice rising, "don't you dare tell me you been turning your back on the Lord. He would never leave you, and you know the truth of that. What have you got to say for yourself?" Mama paused for a breath.

"It is hard, Mama, being married and all," Rosa replied.

"Oh, so you don't have room in your life for Raymond and the Lord both?" Mama clucked her tongue. "No wonder you been looking so poorly these days. You don't choose between your husband and your faith, girl. Would you give up breathing in case Raymond might want all the air for himself?"

"No, Mama." Rosa couldn't help laughing.

"Well, that old Bible is your breath of life, child. Now get back to reading it every morning, like your Grandma Rose did for us. Wouldn't hurt to read it some, night times, too, and times between."

"But Parks . . . ," Rosa began. Mama wouldn't let her finish.

"It will make you strong enough for that man of yours," Mrs. McCauley promised, "maybe even stronger." She paused. "Now, you going to heed what I'm saying?"

"Yes, ma'am. I'll be reading the Good Book every day, all my life, I promise." Rosa said it in a sorry little girl's voice to make her mother laugh, but she meant every single word.

. . .

Parks kept up his work, trying to get conditions changed for blacks in the South and raising money for the Scottsboro Boys. Their court case dragged on for five more years before it was finally over. In 1937, five of the boys were sent to jail for long prison terms. Four others were set free. It was much better than killing them all, but justice had not been done. Things were not fair in Alabama, and thanks to newspapers everywhere, now the world knew it. Activists had learned something, too. Now they knew how a court battle and lots of publicity could change things.

A lot needed to be changed in the South. Blacks could not vote there. The U.S. Constitution said they had the right to, but local people made sure they never tried. If blacks voted, they would elect a governor who was not a KKK member. They would vote against all the Jim Crow laws, too. Blacks would vote for laws fair to all races. Voting meant equality. It meant power.

The people who had power did not want to share it. White supremacists, especially the KKK, made it almost impossible for blacks to register to vote. They attacked colored people heading for the voting booths. They had murdered hundreds of voters, candidates, and community leaders since the Civil War. They did it to scare the blacks away—and it had worked.

"I want to vote for that Franklin Roosevelt to be president again," Rosa told Parks one day. "I like what he has done to help the country out of the depression." Parks nodded without looking up from his newspaper. "I like his wife, Eleanor, too," she said, but Parks wasn't listening.

Rosa wanted to remind him that Eleanor had stood up to the powerful white lady's club when they said Marion Anderson could not sing in Constitution Hall in Washington, D.C. Why? Because she was black. The Daughters of the American Revolution wanted the famous building to stay segregated.

Eleanor had quit the club in anger; then she set it up so Marion could sing right on the steps of the Lincoln Memorial. A crowd of seventy-five thousand people cheered for Marion that night.

Hundreds of thousands cheered for Eleanor when they read the news.

But Rosa could not vote for Roosevelt and his wife that year. There were too many things in her way. She had to make an appointment at the courthouse to register. Then she had to get the time off from her job at the hospital where she worked now. She had to pass a test to prove she could read and write and understand what voting was all about. She had to pay a "poll" tax, too. It was all too much trouble—just the way it was supposed to be.

Rosa's next job was at a nearby air force base. The Maxwell Air Force Base seemed like it was in a different world than Montgomery, Alabama. Here, white supremacists did not rule. Roosevelt had ended segregation in the military, even in the South. For the first time in her life, Rosa could sit anywhere on the bus. She could use any bathroom and drink from any water fountain. She could eat right at the counter or sit at any table in the cafeteria—even if a white person was already sitting at the other end.

When the day was over, though, she had to come home. When she got off of the air force bus at the edge of the base, she had to catch a city bus. There she had to sit in the back again, under the hateful COLORED sign. Things just had to change!

Something did. World War II started. The United States was fighting two enemies. One was Japan, who had bombed Pearl Harbor in Hawaii so they could take over other countries around the Pacific Ocean. The other enemy was Hitler, the leader of Germany. He was a white suprema-cist who felt that nobody but white Germans had the right to live—and he had the power to do something about it. He and his racist govern-ment began killing. They murdered millions and millions of Jews and gays and dark-skinned Gypsys and others. They did not intend to stop killing until they had taken over the world—and made it white. Soldiers from around the world united to stop this evil madman.

Raymond was drafted into the army to fight, and Rosa was afraid for his life. She was angry, too. How dare the country ask him or her brother to risk their lives, if they wouldn't even let them vote?

Now Rosa was determined to register. She went to the office in the winter of 1943, took the test, and waited. Whites were handed their voting certificates right away. "We'll mail it to you," the clerk told Rosa.

Her papers never came.

She took another day off work to see what had happened. "You didn't pass," a white woman in the information booth told her. Rosa remembered the questions. They were tricky, and the writing was confusing, but she was sure she'd done well.

"No," the woman said when Rosa asked to see her test. "You can't see your papers. You don't need to check your answers. You simply didn't pass." The clerk looked over Rosa's shoulder at the next man in line. "Next!" she called out.

Rosa had to move out of the way. She walked

out of the office, her face burning with anger. *It shouldn't be this hard!* she thought. But it was.

Rosa was buttoning up her coat against the cold November wind when a bus pulled up. Rosa glanced in through the windows. The back seats were full. The aisle was crowded with standing blacks. They were even standing on the steps to the back door.

She walked to the front of the bus to pay. When she handed the driver her dime, he glared at her. He was tall and thick, too. He had a mole near his mouth and a mean look in his eye. His skin and voice were both rough.

Rosa glanced back into the bus. There were a few open seats behind the white section. She walked straight to them instead of getting back off the bus and coming in through the crowded rear door.

"Get off my bus!"

Rosa jerked around to see whom the driver was talking to. "You," he glared at her, "get off and go in the way your kind is supposed to."

Rosa didn't stop to think. "I'm already on the

bus," she said. "I don't see any need of making my way up here again. Climbing off. Walking around. Getting on again through that door." She turned to look at the back. "Besides, how can I squeeze through that crowd?"

"If you don't come in the back door," the driver said, "you don't ride my bus."

Rosa just stared at him. She'd paid her money. *It's not fair,* she thought. The driver lurched down the aisle toward her. He grabbed her coat sleeve and pulled her toward the front. *First the voting, and now this?* Rosa's temper flared. She was nearly to the door when she dropped her purse. Instead of leaning over in the aisle, she sat right down in one of the forbidden white seats. Then she took her time and reached calmly over to get her purse. "Get off my bus!" the driver roared.

He didn't take his gun out, but Rosa knew he could. His fists were clenched. "I will," she said, her head high. "But I know one thing. You better not hit me."

As she got to her feet and made her way off the

bus, she heard people, black and white, grumbling. It made Rosa even more furious. They weren't angry because of how the driver had treated her; they were mad because she had made them all late. Most people in Montgomery didn't like the Jim Crow rules. They followed them though, instead of making trouble. Rosa knew she had been like that once, too. She got off the bus and did not get back on. As it roared off down the road, she decided to watch for that driver and never get on his bus again.

Now Rosa was working with the NAACP. Her job was being secretary. There was no pay for this job, but Rosa felt good taking an active part in the fight for equal rights. She took notes at the meetings that the group held in church basements. She got to know all the leaders and the projects they were doing. There was only one other woman member of the Montgomery NAACP. In fact, there were very few black women activists anywhere in 1943. It was lonely for Rosa and hard. Parks was proud of her work, but most of the men

did not take her seriously. They said hurtful things right in front of her. The president of the chapter, E. D. Nixon, knew exactly how much work she was doing for his cause, but one day he told her, "Women don't need to be nowhere but in the kitchen."

"What about me?" Rosa asked, stung by his words.

"I need a secretary," he told her, "and you're a good one." His praise of her work only took some of the hurt away. It was hard being black. It was even harder being black and female. Black women got no respect at all. Rosa knew that, but there was only energy for one fight at a time.

She knew that she was doing a good job of talking to blacks who had been attacked by police or Klansmen. She hated hearing their horrible stories, but she had to listen and take careful notes. Houses with babies in them had been bombed. Blacks had the initials "KKK" burned into their foreheads with acid. Whites sold postcards showing their black victims hanging from trees. It was strictly against the law for whites and blacks to date or fall in love. White men had shot not only their wives but the black men they thought might be getting too friendly with them.

Rosa hated asking the victims to tell her all the details, but her records might someday be used in court. They could supply facts to newspapers for publicity. It might help to change things some-day in Montgomery and the rest of the South. Rosa had heard that there was prejudice against blacks in the North, too. But there weren't any of the Jim Crow laws. Rosa had to work first to change things in her own neighborhood.

Her other NAACP job was much more fun. Rosa was the leader of the youth council. She had always loved children. Rosa had wanted her home to be busy and full of the noise and laughter of little boys and girls. That's the way her Aunt Fannie's house had been. Rosa knew that if God had wanted her to have babies, she would have a houseful by now. Instead, He had given her a chance to teach young blacks through the NAACP. She threw herself into her special "family," teaching them how to be activists.

One project she and her high school kids worked toward was integrating the public library. The rules said that they had to ask for books first at the little COLORED ONLY library. If the books weren't there, the black library would ask the big Montgomery Public Library to send them over. Then, finally, the black students could take them out.

Rosa got her teenagers to go often to the public library and ask, very politely, to borrow books there. "The way we have to do it now takes too long," they explained to the librarians. The library never did change its rules, but the teenagers were learning a way to protest peacefully.

E. D. Nixon was delighted with the work Rosa was doing in his NAACP chapter. He was also the president of the local railroad porter's union. E. D. hired her to work in his union office, too. During the day, she was working as a seamstress again. At night she answered phones and handled the paperwork of activists in the labor movement as well as the NAACP. Rosa was right in the middle of things, and she liked it that way.

Soon she was ready to try to register to vote again. This time E. D. Nixon went along with her to make sure the clerk was fair. Rosa took an extra piece of paper and pencil, too. She copied every test question and her answer. That way, if the clerk tried to tell her she had failed again, Rosa would have a record to prove she was good enough.

Her certificate arrived in the mail, but there was one more step. Rosa had to pay her poll tax at town hall. "That will be a dollar and fifty cents," the clerk said.

Rosa counted out the coins and handed them to the tax collector.

"Oh, no," the tax clerk laughed. "You could have voted every year since you were twenty-one. To vote now, you have to pay the poll tax for every one of those years, too."

It wasn't funny to Rosa. In 1945, $1.50 would buy a meal for a whole family. After all those years . . . it would cost her $16.50 to vote! She gasped and paid it. Though the depression was over and wages had risen, not many blacks could have come up with that much money.

But at last Rosa could vote. The next election was for governor of Alabama. A new man, "Big Jim" Folsom, was running against the old, racist KKK governor. Big Jim was as different as he could be. He talked about equal rights for blacks and for women, too. His enemies called him "nigger lover." They said he was the most dangerous man in America. Rosa was delighted to cast her vote for Big Jim. She was thrilled when he won the election. Surely, big changes were coming to Alabama—and her vote had made a difference!

Rosa's Bus

Rosa and her mother sat in the small apartment watching the flickering picture on their little black-and-white TV set. Mrs. McCauley shook her head slowly. "My, my," she said, then, "Blessed be."

Rosa watched speechless as a little black girl walked right up the steps into a public school. She looked helpless against hundreds of angry whites screaming at her from all sides. Some of them waved threatening fists. Others held angry signs and were shouting at the top of their lungs. It looked as if they would tear the little girl apart before they let her go into their school.

Armed National Guards fought to hold the mob back.

"Who would think the police would protect her?" Mrs. McCauley wondered.

"They have no choice, Mama," Rosa said. She could not take her eyes off the screen. "The Supreme Court ruled it. The schools have to let our people in now." Goosebumps prickled along Rosa's arms. "The police have to make it happen. Like it or not, the schools are integrated."

"'And a little child shall lead them,'" Mrs. McCauley quoted from the Bible.

Now Rosa was the one shaking her head. "It is high time," she said firmly. "It's 1955, Mama. Lincoln freed the slaves ninety years ago."

Rosa thought about her mother, teaching for years and years in shabby little schools, without books, or desks, or screens, or even glass in the windows. How could whites have lied to themselves, saying those black schools were "separate but equal"? The schools were shameful and so were the teachers' salaries. The NAACP had won equal pay for black teachers back in 1945, but the students still had to go to segregated schools. "No more," she told herself. "No more."

"Do you think our Sylvester will come home now?" Mrs. McCauley asked. "My little grand-babies could go to school right here now."

"No, Mama." Rosa said. "Sylvester and his wife feel safer in Detroit." Her brother had moved north when he got back from the war in 1948. Though he was a war hero, racist white Southerners made it clear that, now that he was back in Alabama, he was just a "nigger" again. Sylvester wouldn't stand for it. It was safer for him to leave. Rosa smiled, remembering the two-week visit she had had with him and his wife in Detroit soon after he moved.

"Stay with us in Michigan," he had pleaded. "There're no Jim Crow laws up here."

That part had sounded good, but moving north meant living through bitter winter weather. She'd have to leave her church and the Sunday school classes she taught. Rosa would have to drop her NAACP positions and projects. And blacks in the

North faced prejudice, too. There were lots of jobs they couldn't get, neighborhoods where they couldn't buy a home, and parts of town it was dangerous to walk through. Detroit had its own KKK groups. When Parks said, "I'm not moving to Detroit," Rosa had hugged her brother, his wife, and their two babies, and gone home to Montgomery.

"Just look at those people . . ." Mrs. McCauley stared at the TV. The whites' faces were twisted with rage.

"We've won, Mama. They have to accept it now."

The NAACP had been working to get schools desegregated for years. Rosa had helped behind the scenes with many other plans to challenge the Jim Crow laws. Her work had won the respect of many of the black leaders of the civil rights movement. She had been secretary to the state NAACP as well as the Montgomery branch. Her evenings were spent as an activist. Her Sundays were devoted to the AME Church, where black pastors were urging their congregations to act. Rosa's days were spent sewing for white families. E. D. Nixon had set up one of the sewing jobs with the Durrs.

Virginia Durr was a churchwoman, too—but with a difference. She held integrated prayer circles in her living room with both white *and* black women. Besides paying Rosa to fix her clothes, she invited Rosa into her circle—then became a friend. Mrs. Durr paid dearly for her belief in racial equality. The white husbands of some of her prayer circle ladies took out newspaper ads complaining about her. That didn't stop Mrs. Durr. She kept working with both white and black civil rights activists. It didn't end her friendship with Rosa either. The older woman loaned Rosa books, and they talked about current events, spending many afternoons together.

"Rosa," Mrs. Durr said one day, "would you like to go to the Highlander Folk School this summer?"

The Highlander? Rosa's heart raced at the thought. That famous school taught freedom fighters how to get laws changed. Of course she wanted to go there. She'd be more useful to everybody that way—to E. D., to her youth group, to the NAACP, to her church. . . . *But it costs so much!* Rosa's shoulders fell.

Before she could refuse, Mrs. Durr added, "I heard that a scholarship is available to one black activist from Montgomery. It wouldn't cost you anything."

"I'm not sure, Mrs. Durr," Rosa said. After years of friendship she still could not bring herself to call a white woman by her first name. "It's all the way over in Monteagle, Tennessee. How am I going to get there?"

Virginia Durr could hear the longing in Rosa's voice. "Don't you worry yourself, Rosa. I'm sure the scholarship people will help with the bus fare, too." She wanted this as much as Rosa did. Without telling her friend, Mrs. Durr found someone to pay for the trip. She helped out with suitcases, too, and even bought Rosa her first swimsuit. "You talk to your boss at the department store, Rosa," Virginia said, "and see what Raymond thinks. I'll take care of all the rest."

Rosa's boss liked her. She worked in the basement of the department store, sewing clothes that people had just bought so they would fit perfectly. Then she would use the pressing machine on them. She was careful, dependable, and polite. Her boss knew about her civil rights work, but he didn't care, so long as it didn't affect her job. "My little Miss Rosa at that famous school? You can go, sure enough. But you get yourself back on time, you hear now?"

Getting Raymond's permission was another thing.

"What are you thinking, woman?" He paced around their tidy little apartment. "We don't have money for a fancy school. Leaving, middle of the summer like that, you'll lose your job. Besides, your mama needs you to take care of her."

Rosa explained that the trip was paid for, her boss had agreed, and it was fine with Mrs. McCauley. Someone was taking over her NAACP secretarial job, and dozens of the children in her youth group had told dear Miss Rosa that they would be fine for two weeks. Her Sunday school class was covered, too.

Parks stood and stared out the window. "Rosa," he said firmly, "I don't want you to get more involved." His voice dropped. "It's too dangerous."

There wasn't a good answer for this. Raymond was right. Rosa had been lucky. Many NAACP members had been beaten. Many others had lost their jobs because of their civil rights work. Several of their friends had been killed.

"I am careful, Parks," she said. "This is God's work. It must be done. '. . . not my will, but Thine,'" she quoted. Finally, Parks agreed to let her go, but he didn't like her getting new ideas from new people—and taking on new risks.

Monteagle, Tennessee, is in the Appalachian Mountains. Instead of hot, busy Montgomery streets and the sluggish, red-brown Alabama River, Rosa awoke each morning to birdsong and mountains, cool forests, and clear mountain streams. That change was easy to get used to. It was harder to fit in with the people.

All the whites and blacks called each other "Sister" and "Brother" and by their first names.

Men and women of all ages from many parts of the country took classes together. They ate side by side. They laughed and joked and talked to each other as equals. It was days before Rosa could bring herself to relax and take part. Even then, she spoke quietly. She waited until everyone else had spoken before she said what she thought.

And everyone listened to her.

They wanted to hear all of the horrible stories she had collected of racism and violence in Montgomery. They wanted to hear the NAACP plans—what had worked and what hadn't. They listened to the work she had done with her precious youth council. One of her high school girls had been arrested for refusing to give up her seat on a bus. The police had dragged her off, screaming and crying.

"What happened?" the people at Highlander Folk School asked. "Did you use her court case to start something big like they did in Baton Rouge?" In that Louisiana town, a black had refused to give up his seat on a bus. He was arrested, and all the blacks had banded together.

They'd refused to use the buses at all until the rules were changed. This boycott worked. The bus company lost so much money that even they wanted the change.

"Well," Rosa said, "we talked about it." She told them about Jo Ann Robinson, the head of Montgomery's black Women's Political Council. "She said she could organize a boycott overnight."

"She is a gem!" one of the Monteagle activists said. "We could sure use her in our town."

"We decided not to push this case in court," Rosa said. The crowd around her groaned until Rosa explained why. "The girl had cursed something awful in public. It turned out she was pregnant, too. 'Sides that, her father has a drinking problem. Once the newspapers got a hold of all that, it would have hurt our cause more than help it." Everyone nodded. They all knew how careful you had to be.

As everyone shared their ideas and stories from around the country, Rosa was learning. She learned in the classes, too. The Highlander Folk School had talks on how to organize crowds, how to use newspapers and radio to get publicity, how to speak powerfully in front of groups. And they taught a new way to fight back against Jim Crow laws.

"Just don't go along with what is wrong," they said. "Do not get violent. Act nonviolent instead. Do not even fight back. Simply resist. Stay peaceful." It sounded to Rosa like Jesus' rule about turning the other cheek if someone strikes you. But the idea of using nonviolence to cause political change came from Mahatma Gandhi. He was a great and gentle man in India who worshipped Buddha. Britain had owned all of India and treated the Indians almost as slaves. Gandhi taught the Indians nonviolence. Millions of them simply disobeyed the English rules. English police began beating them, but there were too many. They didn't fight back. They didn't argue. They stayed peaceful.

They clearly hadn't done anything to deserve being beaten in the first place. It made the British feel—and look—very cruel. In shame, they changed the rules and freed India.

"If you organize enough people," the Highlander School teachers said, "and all of you refuse to follow a rule, change will happen."

"My youth group tried something like that," Rosa said. She told how she had organized her high schoolers to protest segregation calmly and politely. "The library didn't change the rules though."

"But look what you did!" They praised her. "All the people in the library had to say 'no' to polite, clean, well-spoken young people. They'll never forget how bad they felt doing it. It will change how they feel about those Jim Crow laws. You just needed to get more students involved and publicity. And remember, nonviolent change takes time."

By the time she left the Highlander School, Rosa had seen how true integration of the races could work. "Parks, you would not believe!" she gushed. "A white woman cooked me my breakfast. And a white man served it to me!" Her husband was glad she was home so she could cook for him.

"Wait until you hear all I've learned!" she cried to E. D. Nixon. He listened carefully to the new ideas for making change happen. Then the NAACP meetings went on, full of men who seldom listened to her.

It was hard for Rosa to remember the beautiful Tennessee landscape when she was back at her job, using the big, hot steam press in the basement of the department store. No one there wanted to hear how wonderful life could be.

But Rosa knew. She carried the ideas and the knowledge with her everywhere. It made her see things differently. She was angrier at the problems—and more determined to try to change them.

One day Rosa went to a lecture by a new, young minister in town, Martin Luther King Jr. He was talking about the Supreme Court decision to end school segregation. "He's something else!" Virginia Durr whispered, as Martin's deep voice began rolling through the little church basement.

"He sure is!" Rosa breathed. They were silent then, astonished. It wasn't just what Martin said, but how beautifully he put the words together that made him so inspiring. It was almost like hearing a poem, or a song, and just as stirring to the soul. Rosa wrote him a note the next day inviting him to join the executive committee of the NAACP. He was busy, but Rosa—and the rest of the world—would soon see a lot of Martin Luther King Jr.

For now, all anybody saw was violence. A black sixteen-year-old boy from Chicago came south to visit his relatives. Emmett Till didn't know anything about being black in the South. He dared to say, "Bye, bye," in a friendly way to a white woman in Mississippi. Within hours, the woman's husband and his brother-in-law were seen kidnapping the boy. A few days later, Emmett's body, horribly beaten, was pulled out of the river. Photos of his broken body and smashed face were printed in newspapers around the world. Rosa could not even look at the pictures without feeling sick to her stomach—and coldly furious.

Somehow, the white Mississippi courts found his murderers not guilty.

Like the case of the Scottsboro Boys years earlier, it was something so awful no one could ignore how bad things were in the South. Most whites were disgusted. Many blacks were too angry to be "good" any longer. They were ready to take action.

On December 1, 1955, Rosa went shopping on her way home from work. She bought a few Christmas presents. At Lee's Cut Rate Drug Store she picked up some aspirin to take later with Coke. Her head ached. Her shoulders ached, too, from working the heavy pressing machine. Her back was sore from standing all day, and her feet were swollen. Her heart was heavy from all of the bad news of the city. She just wanted to get home.

When the bus finally came, Rosa forgot to check who was driving. She dropped her dime in the fare box and chose a seat in the colored section. There were several empty seats left for whites. Rosa double-checked as she finally sat down beside a black man. Across the aisle, two black women were talking. Rosa sighed with relief and sagged against the back of the seat.

Her weary mind drifted as whites got on at the next two stops. At the third bus stop, the final white seat was filled. One white man was left standing. He stood waiting for the blacks to empty the next row of seats for him.

The driver turned around. It was the same man Rosa had sworn never to ride with again—the mean driver who had put her off the bus twelve years earlier. He looked straight at Rosa as he said, "Move, y'all."

Nobody moved.

No one said a word.

"Y'all better make it light on yourselves," the driver snarled.

The two women across from Rosa quietly got to their feet. They kept their eyes down and hurried into the back of the bus to stand in the aisle for the rest of the trip. The man next to Rosa stood and she moved her legs to the side so he could get out.

Rosa took a breath. It was time to decide. Would she go to the back of the bus? Rosa looked at the driver. She was tired of men like him. She was tired of the whole Jim Crow system. She was tired of being a second-rate citizen. This was her chance to make a difference.

Rosa did not stand up. Instead, she slid over to the window. Her Highlander Folk School training had taken over. It would be harder to get her out if she wasn't sitting on the aisle. She sat, calmly gazing at a movie theater. She wasn't seeing the movie posters though. She was seeing her grandfather sitting by the front door, shotgun across his knees. She was seeing the Scottsboro Boys waiting to die, newspaper photos of Emmett Till's broken face, and years of black bodies hung from trees and left dangling. A thought of Sojourner Truth flashed through her mind. She remembered Harriet Tubman's bravery. It was up to Rosa, now. It was her turn. She was filled suddenly with a peaceful calm.

"Are you going to stand up?" The driver loomed over her now, fists ready, his loaded gun bulging in its holster.

Rosa looked straight into his eyes and said, politely, "No."

The Long Walk

Rosa had said, "No." She wouldn't get up. She wouldn't move to the back of the bus. She wouldn't submit to the South's Jim Crow laws any longer. But she had said it with such quiet dignity that the driver could not bring himself to react with force.

"Well," he told her, "I'm going to have you arrested."

Rosa knew what that could mean. She had taken dozens of notes from other blacks who'd been pushed, punched, and pounded with clubs by Montgomery police. They had attacked black people on the streets, in police stations, and in jail. And no policeman had ever lost his job for the abuse he gave to a black. Rosa took another long breath and answered his threat. "You may do that." Quiet. Firm. Polite.

The driver hurried to the front of the bus, grabbed his radio, and called his boss to ask what to do with a lady who wasn't afraid of anything. "You have to get her off that bus," he was told. "Call the police if you have to." The call was made, and the driver got off the bus and stood on the sidewalk, waiting for the police.

Inside the bus, Rosa sat, wondering what would happen next. One by one, the other passengers left. They hurried past her seat without speaking. Some of them she knew, but they wouldn't even meet her eyes. They wanted no part of a scene that might soon turn ugly.

Rosa prayed. Reassuring Bible verses came to her mind. *"Trust ye in the Lord forever,"* she thought, *"for in the Lord is everlasting strength."* She looked out the window. *"The Lord is my shepherd . . .*" She was silently reciting the Twenty-third Psalm when she saw the police arrive.

At first they stood on the curb, talking to the bus driver. One after another they looked in at her. The driver shook his head, and the officers got onto the bus. They both walked back to stand over her.

"Why don't you just stand up?" one of them asked.

Rosa didn't move. "Why do you all push us around?" she answered, thoughtfully.

"I don't know," the policeman said. "but the law is the law and you're under arrest." He picked up her purse. The other officer gathered her shopping bags and walked with her off the bus. Rosa cooperated, sitting quietly in the squad car. They gave her back her belongings, and after talking with the bus driver again, they drove to the police station.

"Why didn't you stand up when the driver asked you to?" one of the officers asked as they drove along.

Rosa simply didn't answer him, and the rest of the ride passed in silence.

"May I have some water," she asked as they entered the police station. "My throat is real dry."

One policeman nodded yes, but as she bent to drink, the other barked, "No. You can't drink no water. Wait 'til you get to jail." Rosa followed the men to the front desk. All around her were policemen, all white, all armed. *How many of them wear KKK sheets in their free time?* Rosa wondered. She was careful to answer their questions honestly, to fill out the forms correctly.

"May I make a telephone call?" she asked. She knew Raymond would be worried by now. She was going to have to find a lawyer. She needed someone there with her, if just to help her get a drink of water.

"No," was the answer. *I do have a right to a phone call,* she thought, *even if I am black.* She looked around. There was not one friendly face in the police station. No one to help her. Now Rosa knew she had to face what was going to happen alone. The police drove her to the jail across town. They walked her up the stairs and into the building. "Leave your purse on the counter," she was told, then, "Empty your pockets." Rosa took out a single tissue. It looked sad and crumpled and helpless on the counter. Rosa's fingerprints were taken, next. A policeman took her photograph, front and side, like any criminal.

A woman jail guard came to walk her to her cell.

"Can I use a telephone?" Rosa asked.

"I'll have to see about that," the matron said, and led her up some stairs. She unlocked an iron mesh door; then they walked down a dim, smelly hall. "Here," she said, showing Rosa into an empty, dark jail cell. She slammed the door closed and walked away.

Rosa stood, stunned. She looked around at the stained walls, bare metal bed, tiny sink, and open toilet, all sitting right in the middle of the cell. No comfort. No privacy. *How could anyone live here?* she asked herself. *How could I . . . ?* The idea was too horrible to think about. Suddenly the matron was back. "There are two girls around the other side," the woman said. "If

you want to go there instead of being in a cell by yourself, I will take you. . . ."

"It doesn't matter," Rosa mumbled, her mind blank.

"Let's go around there," the matron made the decision for her. "Then you won't have to be in a cell alone."

"May I use the telephone?" Rosa asked again, on the way to her new jail cell.

"I'll check," the matron said, and locked Rosa in. Rosa looked at the two black women in the cell with her. One seemed friendly. "Is there anyway I can get a drink of water?" Rosa asked. The woman took a dark metal cup that was hanging above the toilet on a string and pulled it to the water tap. She poured water in from the rusty faucet and offered it to Rosa.

Rosa could only make herself take two swallows. "I got arrested for breaking the bus laws," she explained.

"You married?" the woman asked. When Rosa nodded, she said, "Your husband ain't going to let you stay in here." Then she said, "I got arrested going on two months ago. I been in this cell since then. I got no husband to call, and I can't get in touch with my brothers neither."

"Come out of there." It was the matron, waving to Rosa. With no idea where she was being taken, Rosa followed her out and through the halls. Finally they came to a telephone booth. "Who are you calling?" the guard asked, then handed her a card and a pencil. "Write the number down here."

The matron took the card and dialed the number herself, then stood close enough to hear everything Rosa said.

Mama answered the phone. "I'm in jail," Rosa said, right away. She didn't know how long the guard would let her talk. "No, Mama, I wasn't beaten, but I am in jail." Mrs. McCauley put Raymond on.

"Parks," Rosa said into the phone, "will you come get me out of jail?"

Raymond didn't pause long enough to think. "I'll be there in a few minutes." He already knew what had happened. A friend of his had heard from another friend who was on the bus. It seemed many people knew about Rosa's arrest. Many more would soon hear the news.

Rosa went back to the cell with the guard. Parks wouldn't be there for a while, she knew. He had no car. Getting out of jail meant paying a lot of money for bail, too. Parks would get the bail money back when she showed up in court, but Rosa knew he didn't have that kind of cash ready.

While Rosa sat quietly praying in her cell, a storm of activity had begun in Montgomery. E. D. Nixon had heard of her arrest from his wife. She had heard about it from a neighbor who saw Rosa being taken away by the police. E. D. had tried to call the police station to find out what was going on, but they wouldn't speak to him. He called Fred Gray, one of the two black lawyers in town, but the man wasn't home.

Next, he called Virginia Durr. Her husband was a lawyer, too, and he was white. The police told him what Rosa had been arrested for and how much bail money they wanted for her to go home.

Parks had called around to find someone to

lend him the money. E. D. Nixon offered to meet him with a hundred dollars at the jail. Another friend drove by and gave Parks the keys to his car. "Use it to get Sister Rosa," he said, and walked away.

Rosa was talking with her cell mate when the matron unlocked the door. "You can go now," she said.

Virginia Durr was the first person Rosa saw when the guards let her out through the mesh door. There were tears of worry in her eyes, and her arms were wide open. The friends hugged tightly. In the lobby, E. D. Nixon paid the bail and signed some papers, and then Rosa was free. Parks's hug swept her right off her feet.

They all drove home. Rosa wanted dinner in a clean kitchen. She wanted things to go back to normal. After dinner her friends asked if she wanted to rest for the evening after all that had happened to her. "No," Rosa told them. "I have an NAACP meeting. The children are counting on me."

As E. D. Nixon drove her to the church, he

told her what had been happening since she'd decided to say, "No." He told her she had another decision to make. "I want to use you as a test case against bus segregation. I want to fight this one out in court." He had plans to call the newspapers, Jo Ann Robinson, the NAACP committees, and even the black ministers' council.

"You are our perfect victim," he reminded her, "the one we need." He made a list. "You've never been in trouble in your life. You and Raymond have stayed together. You teach Sunday school, and your work record is good, too. Everyone who knows you, respects you." Rosa smiled when he began talking like that. It sounded like what someone in the Bible had said about Ruth. "All my fellow townspeople know that you are a woman of noble character."

He was right. The newspapers couldn't dig up any dirt to make her sound bad. "Tell me you'll do it." E. D. urged.

"I'll have to think about it," she said. "And I'll have to ask Parks."

◦ ◦ ◦

"Rosa, the white folks will kill you," Parks said. Her mother was horrified, too. If she was in the papers in a fight to desegregate Montgomery, the police would target Parks. There was no telling what the Ku Klux Klan would do. She would lose her job, they all knew that. Her family needed that money.

Besides, Rosa had always lived quietly. She, like many people, believed that it was in bad taste for women to be famous. Proper ladies at that time had their names in the newspaper only twice; once when they were born, and once when they died. Otherwise they never drew attention to themselves. If Rosa agreed to this, her picture would be in the papers all of the time, like the Scottsboro Boys—or like poor dead Emmett Till. But Rosa knew how valuable she could be to the cause of civil rights. She talked it over with Mama and Parks and her friends. She thought about what she had learned at the Highlander School and seen in the streets of Montgomery. She prayed for guidance.

By nine o'clock that night, E. D. Nixon, the

Durrs, Parks, and Mama were sitting with Rosa in her living room around the table her great-grandfather had built. "With your permission," E. D. said to Rosa, "we can break down segregation on the buses with your case."

Rosa had already said, "No," once this day, on the bus. Now she took a deep breath and said a firm, "Yes."

Immediately they began planning. "It will go all the way to the Supreme Court," Mr. Durr said. "It's going to cost a lot of money." He thought a minute, then told them of an NAACP legal defense fund headed by the young civil rights lawyer, Thurgood Marshall. They decided that Fred Gray would be Rosa's lawyer for this case. Clifford Durr offered to handle the press and advise Rosa behind the scenes.

Exhausted, Rosa went to bed.

She was the only one who got any sleep that Thursday night. Fred Gray went home and called Jo Ann Robinson. She called her friends in the Women's Political Council. They met and agreed to call for a boycott of Montgomery's buses starting Monday morning. At midnight, Jo Ann wrote a boycott note. "Another Negro woman has been arrested and put in jail because she refused to get up out of her seat on the bus and give it to a white person." It went on to ask "every Negro to stay off the buses Monday in protest of the arrest and trial. Don't ride the buses to work, to town, to school, or anywhere . . ."

"You can afford to stay out of school for one day," Jo Ann went on. "If you work, take a cab, or walk, but please stay off the buses. Don't ride the buses to work, to town, to school, or anywhere on Monday."

Her friends printed thirty-five hundred copies of it on half sheets of paper. Early Friday morning, they drove them to all the black elementary, junior high, and high schools in Montgomery. That way, every single black child in town would take the note home for his or her family to read. The fliers were dropped off at homes and churches, too.

E. D. Nixon called the newspaper. He told them about Rosa and the boycott and said he wanted a front-page story. At five in the morning, he called the Reverend Ralph Abernathy, minister of the powerful First Baptist Church of Montgomery. When he sounded interested, eighteen other ministers were called and invited to a meeting that very night at the church by the state capitol building. It was the Dexter Avenue Church, where Martin Luther King Jr. was the new minister.

About that time, Rosa was getting up. First, she read the Friday newspaper. Her story was on page nine. Then she called the brothers of the friendly woman she'd met in jail and told them to go and get her out. Finally, she went to work. Instead of riding a bus, she took a cab. "I didn't think you would be here," her boss said. While she was quietly stitching in the basement, E. D. Nixon was meeting with another reporter, giving him "the hottest story you've ever written."

At lunch Rosa went to Fred Gray's law office. She'd spent plenty of time at the lawyer's office before on NAACP business, but she'd never seen it like this. People hurried through the door to ask about the boycott then ran out to spread the word. The phones rang endlessly. Messages and notes lay scattered about.

After work, Rosa went to the Dexter Avenue Church. Fifty of Montgomery's black leaders—ministers, NAACP officials, businessmen—were crowded into the basement. They heard her story then discussed what to do about the boycott plan. Some wanted to support it; others didn't. Most of the ministers agreed to talk about it in their churches on Sunday. Afterward, Rosa, Martin Luther King, and Ralph Abernathy stayed behind with a few others. Together, they wrote a new flier like Jo Ann Robinson's. This one added a call for everyone to come to a big meeting on Monday night at the Holt Street Baptist Church.

On Sunday morning, Rosa read the new leaflet, printed on the front page of the newspaper. Black churchgoers heard about the plan in their churches. Everyone knew about the boycott in honor of Rosa's trial on Monday—but would they ride the buses anyway?

* * *

Five hundred people crowded around the town hall Monday morning, cheering for Rosa as she walked up the steps. They were Rosa's friends and many, many more blacks there to support their "Sister Rosa" in her battle. "They've messed with the wrong one now!" one of her Youth Council girls cried. Soon the whole crowd was chanting it. They knew Rosa, and they all knew how strong and good she was.

They all knew what the streets looked like, too, this morning. It had been exciting, seeing thousands of blacks walking to work. Some carried boxes and bags, others briefcases, but not one of them rode the buses. Whites sat tall behind the bus drivers, but, under the COLORED sign, there were only empty seats. Boys raced beside the buses, cheering. A thrilling knowledge of new power grew all day in Montgomery, as blacks saw what they had done, working together.

Things went just as expected in the courtroom. The bus driver lied and said there was another seat where she could have sat in the colored section. Two white women lied, too, swearing that the bus driver was right. In the end, the judge banged his gavel and declared Rosa guilty of breaking the Jim Crow law.

The crowd outside groaned loudly when they heard the verdict. Rosa was a convicted criminal now and had to pay a ten-dollar fine. No one wanted to go home. They didn't want it to end. The boycott had to go on, they decided. E. D. Nixon, Fred Gray, and Ralph Abernathy named a new committee, the Montgomery Improvement Association. This new MIA committee met with a group of ministers that afternoon, trying to shame everyone into helping with the boycott. It wasn't working until Martin Luther King Jr. stood up.

"I'm not a coward," his deep voice rang out. He declared that he wanted the boycott and didn't mind who knew it. For his courage and leadership, he was made president of the MIA.

That night thousands and thousands of African Americans crowded around the church. All the chairs in the meeting hall were filled.

There wasn't any room left to stand either by the time Martin Luther King took the pulpit. Loudspeakers carried his praise of Rosa out into the street. Applause floated over Montgomery, then silence as King's words thrilled the crowd.

"There comes a time that people get tired," he began. "For many years we have shown amazing patience," he said, his deep voice rolling like a prophet's. "We have sometimes given our white brothers the feeling that we liked the way we were treated." Never again, he said, will we be "patient with anything less than freedom and justice!" His words were inspired, and they inspired the audience to endless waves of applause.

"If you will protest courageously and yet with dignity and Christian love," King said, "when the history books are written in future generations, historians will pause and say, 'There lived a great people—a black people—who injected new meaning and dignity into the veins of civilization. . . .'" When he was done, Martin walked across the stage to hug Rosa, and the crowd went wild. Finally Ralph Abernathy took the microphone and challenged everybody to go on with the boycott as long at it took to force the laws to change. Everyone cheered.

Then everyone walked. Or they caught a ride with a neighbor. They organized black taxis. Churches collected money and bought station wagons. Rosa helped plan stops for these church wagons as they drove the streets, from homes to schools and stores and businesses. Weeks passed.

The news of the Montgomery bus boycott spread across America. It gave courage to blacks everywhere. It made racist whites nervous. Then it made them angry. The police became more violent. So did the KKK. Many new members joined the Klan, frightened by how powerful the blacks seemed to be getting. To get back at Rosa and the Montgomery Improvement Association, people spread lies that she had been under NAACP orders to break the law that day on that bus. They said it was all a plot by the Communists. Or the Jews. Rosa and Raymond both lost their jobs. The press could not find any facts to make Rosa look bad though. Months passed, and the blacks of Montgomery kept walking.

People from around the world sent money and packages of new shoes to help. Newspapers sent photographers. Whites began driving to their maids' homes to fetch them. Letters of support came from everywhere. So did threats. Strangers on the phone told Rosa they were going to kill her. Raymond was wild with worry. He drank to forget his fears. Rosa found her strength in prayer. Letters threatened her and the other boycott leaders, too. A bomb was set off in Martin Luther King Jr.'s house. No one there was hurt, and the blacks kept walking.

Seasons passed, and the bus company finally stopped running most of the buses. Without the black passengers' money, they couldn't afford to buy gasoline anymore. The company—and the city—were furious. They charged Rosa and all the other leaders with breaking a law that said people couldn't boycott. A picture of Rosa Parks being fingerprinted again was on the front page of the *New York Times*. They called her a "freedom fighter."

She was asked to speak at schools and churches and meetings around the country, in places like New York, San Francisco, and the Highlander Folk School in Tennessee. She met famous people like Eleanor Roosevelt. Rosa's speaking fees helped pay to organize the boycott, and traveling seemed almost safer than staying home. Her marriage was in tatters, her job gone, her stomach raw with ulcers, and death threats still came in daily. Reverend Abernathy's house was bombed. Martin Luther King's house had been bombed again, too. So had three black churches. A white church whose minister had said he agreed with the boycott was bombed, too. Still, the blacks kept walking.

On November 13, Martin Luther King Jr. told the MIA that the Supreme Court of the United States had ruled that segregation on the Montgomery buses was against the U.S. Constitution. "Don't stop the boycott until the court order gets to Montgomery," the MIA leaders told everyone. The papers arrived on December 20. They had been walking for a year and sixteen days.

The next morning, blacks got back on the buses. They sat wherever they wanted to. Together they had challenged a law and changed the course of history—and Rosa had shown them how.

Marching On

"Rosa, the white folks are going to kill you." Parks had said it over and over before she agreed to go ahead and lead the boycott.

The boycott was over, but the danger wasn't. People began shooting at blacks in town. They fired a shotgun into Martin Luther King's house. More bombs exploded. There were threatening calls at the Parks's home almost every night. "I'm going to kill you, nigger," they said—and worse. Racists even stopped Rosa on the street to say, "You better watch out. . . ." Parks started keeping a gun nearby when they went to bed. The tension made Rosa's ulcers flare painfully, and arthritis added to her stress. Rosa's mother started talking to her friends on the phone for hours in the evenings just so the line was busy when racists tried to call her daughter.

Rosa was such a famous "troublemaker" that she knew she would never get another job working for whites in Montgomery. Her fame was a problem in the local NAACP, too. It was Rosa whom Martin Luther King kept praising in his national speeches. It was Rosa who was invited to speak and travel. And it was Rosa whom reporters wanted to interview. Her friends, E. D. Nixon, Ralph Abernathy, and many others, grew jealous of all the attention she was getting. After all, she was just a woman. And hadn't they done all the work of organizing the boycott?

"You're our superstar," they teased Rosa, knowing how much that would sting the quiet woman. They said some cruel things about Raymond, too. The death threats continued. There was no money coming into the house. Raymond had become terribly depressed about his life and hers.

Rosa was not a complainer, but she finally had to tell someone about her troubles. She chose her brother, Sylvester. He had told her cousins who lived near him in Detroit. When one of them, Thomas, invited her to come and live there, Rosa was ready. "We're leaving," she told everyone.

Now, suddenly, all of her friends were sorry they had acted so badly. "I didn't mean all that," she heard. "You knew I was just funnin' with you, right?" and "We're sure going to miss y'all." E. D. Nixon collected eight hundred dollars as a going away gift. That plus three hundred dollars that Thomas sent made the move possible. In the summer of 1957, Rosa sold her furniture— all but her great-grandfather's table—and moved her little family to Detroit, Michigan.

Parks, Rosa, and her mother settled into an upstairs apartment Sylvester had found for them. Barbers had to get a license to work in Detroit, so Parks went back to barber school. Mama settled in, with her son, Sylvester, and thirteen grandchildren nearby.

Rosa loved playing with all of her nieces and

nephews. She sewed for them and babysat. She took in sewing for neighbors, too. It wasn't enough for her. Rosa might have left Montgomery behind, but she was still a "freedom fighter." There were many civil rights battles left to fight. She joined the local NAACP to see what she could do to help. Rosa was still getting invitations to speak around the country. She felt she had to say yes.

After she gave a speech in Boston Massachusetts, a man offered her a job running the dining room at the Hampton Normal and Agricultural Institute in Virginia. It would mean being part of a black college. The money was good. Rosa thought that Raymond could work there, too, so she said yes and went to start the job. "I'm getting work at the barber school," Parks told her, "and I don't want to move again."

"I don't want to be leaving my little grand-babies," Mama said. "Besides, I'm not feeling so fine these days."

Suddenly Rosa was alone, far from everyone who mattered to her. One day, a package came. It was from Martin Luther King Jr.! Rosa tore it open. It was his new book, *Stride Toward Freedom*. She flipped open the cover. Martin had signed it to her and written a lovely note inside. It was like having her dear friend right beside her again.

"Look, look!" Rosa ran to show the workers in her kitchen.

As soon as she had a chance, Rosa sat down with the book in a soft chair in the college parlor. She couldn't wait to read her friend's words. The room was empty and silent, except for a radio playing quietly nearby.

"We repeat, Martin Luther King has been stabbed." Rosa jumped from her chair at the news on the radio. "He has been taken to the hospital. Nothing is known of his condition." Rosa dropped to her knees and began praying, sobbing aloud and whimpering to God to spare her friend. Others in the college heard her. "Easy, Rosa," they tried to calm her.

Someone turned the radio up. "Minutes ago," the announcer was saying, "a woman stabbed the civil rights leader as he signed books at a department store in Harlem, New York." Rosa clutched the book tighter, and wailed.

"I'll call the hospital and see how he is for you," someone else offered. "They'll tell me when I say it's Rosa Parks wants to know."

"He is in the operating room," was the first report. Soon it was, "Martin is out. He lost some ribs, some of his breastbone, and a lot of blood, but he'll survive."

Now Rosa prayed again, a prayer of thanks. It was a sober prayer. Martin hadn't even been attacked by an angry racist. It was just some lady who went crazy for a moment. He happened to get in the way of her knife. He could have been hit by a truck instead. Or lightning could have killed him. Suddenly Rosa knew that Martin Luther King Jr.—and all of the other people in her life—were fragile. She missed them all.

After that Christmas, Rosa moved back to live with Raymond and her mama in Detroit.

A cousin invited Rosa to join the small Saint Matthew AME Church in Detroit. The church welcomed her, not just as the famous civil rights activist, but as a devout Christian. For Rosa that didn't just mean sitting in a pew on Sunday. "Do you need a Sunday school teacher?" she asked, and, "How else can I help?" Soon Rosa was a stewardess in the church, helping with baptisms and other ceremonies.

"Sister Rosa, will you serve as deaconness?" When the call came from her minister several years later, Rosa didn't hesitate. A deaconness's job is to weave connections between the church and people. It was the highest honor a woman could hold in an AME church. On Sundays Rosa wore a special, simple dress and black bonnet. She called on the sick, ran clothing drives, visited mental hospitals and prisons, and helped print the church bulletin. When there was need, she organized aid for anyone in the neighborhood who had trouble. Churchpeople would gather to help, just like little Rosa and her family had back in Pine Level.

The people were nice where she worked, too. Rosa's job was sewing in a factory in downtown

Detroit. The hours were long, but the pay good. "My name is Elaine Steele," a new girl said from the next sewing machine one day. "What's yours?"

When Rosa answered, the sixteen year old cried, "You're not THE Rosa Parks, are you really?" Elaine chattered to her endlessly over the next few days, asking about the boycott and the Montgomery Improvement Association and Martin.

"Elaine, dear, don't you think you should be sewing instead of talking?" Rosa often interrupted the cheery chatter. Elaine would laugh and be silent—but only for a few minutes.

A few days later, the boss had a talk with Elaine. "You don't work fast enough," he said. "You're fired."

Rosa missed her at work. She liked the girl's high spirits, and they kept in touch as the girl went back to high school. At night Rosa was busy, as always, with civil rights groups. Now she became active in the local Southern Christian Leadership Council, an organization headed by Martin Luther King Jr. In 1963, she went to an SCLC convention in Birmingham,

Alabama. She was sitting right next to the stage when a white man jumped out of the audience and slammed a fist into Martin's face. Everyone started screaming.

Martin didn't hit back. He had always preached nonviolence to people, and now he acted on his beliefs. He dropped his hands to his sides and started talking calmly to his attacker. The man was so surprised, he forgot to hit Martin again. Others pulled him away.

Rosa sat, stunned. How she loved this gentle man! As soon as it was safe, she hurried backstage to give him Coke and aspirin for his headache.

Martin Luther King Jr. and other leaders had asked everyone to gather for a huge, peaceful "March on Washington for Jobs and Freedom." It would be the biggest civil rights march ever, and the publicity would be wonderful for their cause—but only if it stayed nonviolent. To make sure things went smoothly, they decided to hold a smaller march in Detroit first.

Thousands of blacks paraded down Detroit's

main street. As they marched, they sang to keep their spirits up, as black fieldhands had done for hundreds of years. Sometimes they chose the old hymns, like "Oh, Freedom," "Amazing Grace," and "We Shall Overcome." Other times, they took old favorites like "We Are Bound for the Promised Land" and changed it to "We Are Bound for the Freedom Land." It made Rosa think about her days in the cotton fields and her grandparents' lives as slaves. They had come so far! Together there was no end to what they could do.

Rosa and Martin spent most of the day together. She was listening when he gave his famous speech, stirring the whole world with his words, "I have a dream . . ." Rosa was overjoyed by the success of that march in Detroit.

The march on Washington, D.C., was a disappointment to Rosa. They sang the same songs. Everyone stayed calm and nonviolent. The press was there. The crowds were huge. Even the weather was nice. But there was no place there for Rosa—or for any other woman. Not as a speaker. Not sitting on the stage. Not even marching in the streets. It seemed that no matter how many years they'd fought alongside their men, black women were not welcome.

It's not fair! Rosa's old anger bubbled up again. A few of the men saw what they had done and decided to have Rosa introduced. That was all. She could stand up, the crowd could cheer, and then she'd have to sit down and be quiet while men spoke. Another plan gave the women a march of their own, far away from the TV cameras and the White House.

Rosa returned home, full of angry energy. When President Kennedy was killed, she was angrier still. What was happening to the world? Rosa was ready to be a freedom fighter again. It didn't seem that she could help the cause by marching. Now she decided to try to get more blacks elected to offices. When she got back to Detroit, she heard about a young black lawyer, John Conyers Jr. He was a civil rights activist who wanted to run for the U.S. Congress from Michigan. "You don't know me," he told everyone, "but I stand for jobs, justice, and peace."

"I like your ideas," she told him. "Could you use some help?" Conyers was glad to have Rosa on his side. She told Martin about the young politician. Reverend King came to Detroit to give a speech and tell everyone to vote for John.

John Conyers was elected. One of the first things he did was hire Rosa to work in his office. She was being paid to do what she'd always done for free in NAACP offices: work to help people of color. John's office found housing and jobs for homeless people, helped encourage voter registration, and fought prejudice wherever they could.

Things seemed to be falling into place at last. President Lyndon Johnson signed a Civil Rights Act to enforce voting rights. It said that if a state kept some of its citizens from voting, the federal government could send soldiers in to make sure everyone's rights were protected—especially blacks.

White supremacists were furious. Racists in Selma, Alabama, were still keeping blacks from voting. Nonviolent protests were planned in town, with lots of publicity to shame people into following the laws. Protestors sang as they sat downtown. They sang as they marched through the town. Through it all, they stayed peaceful. The white police and the Alabama National Guardsmen did not.

Right in front of TV cameras, the police attacked peaceful marchers on a bridge over the Alabama River. There was nowhere to run from the police on horseback. They swung clubs, sprayed stinging tear gas, and used electric sticks to shock everyone they could reach. The marchers stayed nonviolent through the whole thing. TV stations around the country stopped their programs to show the horrifying scene. Now everyone knew how ugly racial hatred was in the South.

Martin called Rosa to see if she would take part in another march to Montgomery. He and the SCLC were going to march again, right away. All of Alabama was ashamed by the cruelty the world had seen. They would not dare attack them again. Martin wanted to test whether the governor of the state had learned to control his troops and police.

Rosa said yes to help her old friend. He was right, and she knew it. This time the entire march was peaceful, but it felt strange to be back in Montgomery. Rosa had thought things had changed there. True, the buses were integrated now, but angry white crowds were still screamed "nigger" at her. Rosa was threatened with death, just like before. The marchers this time were younger activists. Many had no idea who Rosa was. They hadn't saved space for her to march on the street. All of the risks she had taken seemed forgotten.

She wasn't alone in her frustration. Many blacks thought change was taking too long. Some of them began to question Martin Luther King Jr.'s nonviolent way of protest. Even Rosa thought it would be better to fight back sometimes. The whites had been ashamed by how they looked to the world. They were angry with the changes they'd been forced to make. Now they were nervous because they thought the blacks might revolt. That made them even angrier. Blacks were angry and nervous, too. Something big was going to happen.

It was hot in Detroit on July 23, 1967. Tempers were hot, too. At four in the morning, police raided a bar in a black section of town, and all the frustration broke loose. When they came out, an angry black mob had formed. They beat the police, and then the crowd went wild. Cars were turned over. Fires were set. Store windows were broken. Thieves went right in and helped themselves to whatever they wanted. When the sun came up, huge areas of Detroit were in flames.

But the worst had just started. Rioting went on for eight days. Whole apartment buildings burned, then whole blocks. Detroit did not have enough police or fire trucks, so the president sent in the U. S. Army. The rioters were filled with a crazy rage. They attacked anyone and anything, destroying whatever they could. More troops were sent in. In the end, it took five thousand soldiers to bring peace to the city.

"Sister Rosa," the call came from the church, "what are we going to do? Five thousand people are homeless. Where do we start?"

"Oh, Rosa," Parks told her when he got back from his barbershop, "everything is gone. They stole all my tools. They tore my barbershop apart. Then they burned what was left. What are we going to do?"

Some people said the blacks had rioted to get equal pay and jobs and treatment everywhere.

"Those hooligans?" Rosa spat. "Those rioters weren't freedom fighters. They were common thieves and criminals. They hid under the cover of night and smoke to do the nastiest things they could think of. And just look what they've done to our city."

Nonviolence? That seemed just a dream. Progress? All lay in ashes.

The stink of smoke and charred wood hung over Detroit for weeks. It took months and months to sort out the damage: fifty million dollars' worth. They were still clearing rubble away eight months later.

On April 4, 1968, Rosa and her mother were at home listening to a preacher on the radio. Suddenly the announcer broke in. "Attention, please. Martin Luther King Jr. has been shot in the head." Moments later he came back. "He is gone. Martin Luther King Jr. is dead."

Rosa wept along with the rest of the world. She had lost a dear friend and role model. The world had lost a great leader who wanted only peace and justice.

Riding the Bus

Civil rights activists everywhere were sad after Martin Luther King Jr.'s death. They were tired from years of fighting for equality. They were shaken by the summer of black riots in cities around the country. And there did not seem to be another leader who could inspire them all the way Martin had.

Rosa was sad, too, tired, shaken, and lonely for her old friend. She went back to Detroit after Martin's funeral. At sixty, her health was bad. Now she had heart trouble as well as ulcers. Her family's health was bad, too. During the early

1970s Rosa learned that Parks, Mama, and Sylvester all had cancer.

At first, Rosa kept working at John Conyers's office. Young Elaine Steele, now a married mother with two children, worked in the same building as Rosa. She drove her old friend to and from work. Rosa was still helping with the local NAACP and giving speeches when asked. She was answering hundreds of letters a week from people around the world. Rosa's good works with Saint Michael's AME Church inspired everyone there—and it kept her inspired, too.

Over the years, her family grew sicker. At last she had to make a choice, just as she'd had to in high school. Once again she put her life on hold and spent her time nursing others. In 1977, Raymond died. Rosa had lost her best friend. It was her husband who had insisted she finish her education. It was his example as an activist that had changed her entire life. And Parks had stayed with her even when he did not like what she was doing. His death was a terrible loss. Three months later, Rosa's brother died. Rosa's Mama died in 1979.

Rosa was exhausted and alone. She had lived almost seventy years—and what was there to show for it? One courageous act on a bus. Hundreds of speeches. Thousands of marches. Millions of phone calls answered. Billions of stitches sewn. Where was it all now? The world seemed barely changed. And she had so wanted to make a difference!

Slowly Rosa climbed from her valley of the shadow of darkness. Her faith in God helped. Her church friends helped. The people and her regular job at John Conyers's office helped. Most of all, Elaine Steele helped. She had become like a daughter to childless Rosa.

All of her life, Rosa had said yes. Whenever she was asked to give a speech, or go to a meeting or even answer a piece of mail, she did it gladly. An older woman now, Rosa did not have much energy left, but still she said yes. Elaine Steele helped her by saying no.

"No, I'm sorry, Mrs. Parks cannot speak to you," Elaine told writers and reporters. "I will answer any questions you have." "No," she told clubs and schools, "Mrs. Parks cannot give a speech for you." She even told Rosa, "No, you cannot answer all of these letters yourself. We'll find a secretary to help you."

It was what Rosa needed. Now she could use what energy she had left in ways she wanted to. All the civil rights battles had not been won. Things still weren't fair for blacks in America, and new white supremacist groups were springing up every day. *It's not fair!* Rosa thought to herself. *And, thank the Lord, I still have time to do something about it.*

Rosa prayed about what she could do to help. She talked with Elaine Steele. Together they made a grand plan. Rosa had always loved teenagers—and they had loved her. She was a special friend to her NAACP Youth Council teenagers, her Sunday school students, her nieces and nephews, and children from every neighborhood she'd ever lived in. Teenage Rosa had watched Parks's courage as a freedom fighter—and it had changed her life forever.

Who was showing children today? Rich

children could go to college, of course. Inner-city children—especially children of color—did not have so many chances to learn. But Raymond hadn't even graduated from elementary school—and look what he had done. What if someone took an interest in the poor city students of color? At an age when most women finally just take it easy, Rosa decided, once again, to act. She would focus on the kinds of teenagers whose anger had fueled the Detroit riots.

If only they could see what Rosa had seen. They could do so much with all that energy if they were trained as activists. First, of course, they would have to bring their school work up. There was so much to do!

Rosa and Elaine bubbled over with ideas for their new cause. In 1987, they started the Rosa and Raymond Parks Institute for Self Development for inner-city children. The teenagers signed up to work with the institute for a full year, learning leadership skills. They followed a strict code of behavior, like Rosa had done at Miss White's school. They learned how to reach out into their community, the way Rosa had at the Highlander Folk School. They polished their reading and writing skills along with the manners they would need to work well with people. They practiced community activism by teaching computer skills to the elderly and other projects.

Every year, the institute took a busload of teenagers on a "Pathways to Freedom" trip. The Pathways riders had to promise not to smoke or drink. There was no TV or radio. They ate healthy foods and prayed to their God. They didn't mind all the rules. They got to travel thousands of miles across America and even into Canada, visiting places where the battles for civil rights had been fought. Day by day they saw where people of color—people just like them—had made a difference. Whenever she could, Rosa went along on these trips.

She was reaching out to children in other ways. Rosa and Jim Haskins, an award-winning children's nonfiction writer, wrote a book for children about her life. *Rosa Parks: My Story* came out in 1992. They wrote a picture book too, called,

I Am Rosa Parks. Next, she and a friend, Gregory J. Reed, wrote a small book called *Quiet Strength.* Published in 1994, it is full of her faith and experiences. Through her books, Rosa could talk to millions of people without ever leaving her home.

"Hey!" a young man's voice rang out in Rosa's house one evening that year.

"Yes? Who's there?" Rosa called. She came downstairs in her robe to see what had happened. It sounded like someone had fallen.

It was a trap, in fact, and eighty-one-year-old Rosa had fallen for it.

"You are one lucky old lady!" the black stranger lied. "I just chased away a robber." Rosa could smell the whiskey on his breath as he stepped closer, demanding, "I should get a reward. Three, maybe four dollars?"

Rosa told him that her purse was upstairs and went to get it. The robber followed her into her bedroom. "I want all the money you got in there!" he said.

"No," Rosa told him, "that's not right." The

man punched her in the face over and over, while Rosa screamed for him to stop. Then he threw the frail old woman onto the bed and shook her until she cried, "Take it! Take the money."

He left her on the bed, sobbing and bleeding. He took all the money she had—$103—and ran away into the night. Rosa called Elaine Steele's number from the bedside phone. Elaine came, then the police, then an ambulance. All of them were upset that gentle old Rosa had been mugged in her own home. The newspapers raged about it. The mayor was furious.

Rosa, herself, was sickened by the violence. But she was worried, too. What if people judged all young black men by the actions of this one? "I pray for this young man," she said, "and the conditions in this country that have made him this way." She tried to tell people that children today are strong and good. Rosa knew what she was talking about.

Besides the thousands of children she'd come to know in her institute programs, Rosa was reading hundreds of letters from young fans. Elaine

Steele had shared this special mail with Rosa. A year after her attack, Rosa published many of the letters, and her answers, too, in a book called *Dear Mrs. Parks: A Dialogue with Today's Youth.*

In the summer of 1996, Rosa made her last Pathways bus trip. Her health was failing, but her fame was not. President Clinton awarded her the Presidential Medal of Freedom. There is no higher honor a U.S. citizen can be given.

Three years later, in January of 1999, Rosa was introduced by President Clinton to Congress. One by one, every senator and representative stood in her honor, clapping. On June 6 President Clinton awarded her the Congressional Gold Medal of Honor.

A new Rosa Parks Museum and Library has been built in Montgomery, Alabama. Visitors there can learn about Rosa and the civil rights movement. Every day, buses drive past, integrated buses where whites and blacks sit side by side.

Other buses head out from the Rosa and

Raymond Parks Institute for Self Development in Detroit. The "National Pathways" trips carry teenagers along the route of the Underground Railroad, where Harriet Tubman led slaves to their freedom. "Regional Pathways" students might travel to West Virginia, where John Brown's slave revolt helped to trigger the Civil War. Another bus might go to see the bridge in Selma, Alabama, where racist brutality shocked the world. Or students might go to Montgomery to see where Rosa herself had helped trigger the civil rights era in America. Every year the buses explore different places where civil rights history was made.

So far, more than five thousand children have gone on these freedom rides. Those buses are still running today. Rosa knows that the life of every child on them will be changed. Millions of other kids have learned Rosa's story of life-long action from books by her and about her.

Someday in the future these young people will see something that they know is wrong. When they think, *It's not fair,* they'll know how to change things, thanks to Rosa Parks.

For Further Reading

You can read about Rosa Parks in four books she helped to write:

1. *Rosa Parks: My Story,* by Rosa Parks and Jim Haskins. New York: Dial, Penguin Putnam Books for Young Readers, 1992. This book for middle-grade readers tells about Rosa Parks' early years.

2. *I Am Rosa Parks,* by Rosa Parks and Jim Haskins. New York: Dial Books for Young Readers, Penguin Books, 1997. This easy-to-read book has illustrations by Wil Clay.

3. *Dear Mrs. Parks: A Dialogue with Today's Youth,* by Rosa Parks and Gregory J. Reed. New York: Lee and Low, 1996. Reading this collection of letters from kids and Rosa Parks's answers feels like having a chat with the famous woman.

4. *Quiet Strength,* by Rosa Parks and Gregory J. Reed. Michiagan: Zondervian Publishing House, 1994. This is a heartfelt explanation of Rosa's faith and how it shaped and guided her actions.

5. *A Picture Book of Rosa Parks,* by David A. Adler, illustrated by Robert Casilla. New York: Holiday House, 1993. This is a simple telling of Mrs. Parks's story, beautifully illustrated.

Adults will enjoy reading the excellent biography, *Rosa Parks* by Douglas Brinkley, a Lipper/ Viking Book, Viking, Penguin Putnam Inc., New York, 2000. This detailed book includes a great deal of information about the times and personalities of the civil rights era.